THE DANCE OF INNER PEACE

Look for these forthcoming books by Rosalee Sirgany:

IT HAS ALWAYS BEEN THUS
A Revised Look at
A Course in Miracles

GLIMPSES INTO THE SPIRITUAL REALM
A Collection of Aphorisms and Insights

THE

DANCE

OF

INNER

PEACE

A Journey Into the Spiritual Realm

Love & Light,
Rosalee
Sirgany

By

ROSALEE SIRGANY

to let your spirit soar

Golden Eagle
Publications
Miami, Florida

THE DANCE OF INNER PEACE

A Journey Into the Spiritual Realm

Golden Eagle
Publications
P. O. Box 161011
Miami, Florida 33116-1011 USA

Phone: 305-595-4002
Website: www.goldeneaglespirit.com

If you are unable to order this book from your local bookseller, you may order directly from the publisher. Quantity discounts for organizations are available. Call 1-800-825-1553, toll-free.

Library of Congress Catalog Card Number: 99-96433
Cataloging-in-Publication Data

Sirgany, Rosalee
The dance of inner peace : a journey into the spiritual realm / by Rosalee Sirgany. --1st ed.
p. cm.
ISBN: 0-9673597-5-9
1. Sirgany, Rosalee. 2. Spiritual biography.
3. Guides (Spiritualism) 4. Reincarnation.
5. Dreams--Religious Aspects. I. Title.
BP610.N48S57 1999
299.93′092 99-96433

10 9 8 7 6 5 4 3 2 1
Printed on acid-free paper in the United States of America.

To my Mom and Dad, Yvonne and Richard, for their loving support and encouragement,

To all those in all dimensions who have touched my life and helped to make this book possible,

And to you, the reader, may this book assist you in your own personal journey into the spiritual realm.

I love you all.

Acknowledgments

My sincerest thanks and appreciation go to Jeffrey Brock, my dear friend and editor at Golden Eagle Publications, for his expertise, assistance and loving support.

I also thank Robertson Adams, along with Ana Balzan and Lisa Spilka for their wonderful work on the book cover.

My grateful appreciation goes to Glen Rostant and Wayne Espinola at Cloud 9 Solutions for their superb help with the interior graphics.

I also thank my brother Richard (Rick) Sirgany for the author's photo and my brother Steve Sirgany for his loving encouragement.

Many thanks also go to Van Martin and Robert (Chino) Morales for their capable assistance with the computer.

Special thanks also go to Russel Rogg for his encouragement and support of my sharing this work.

My deep appreciation goes to Rebecca Ross, Lisa Fox, Rachel Kraemer, Michael Kraemer, and all of the others who have, through their friendship and encouragement, helped to make this book possible.

Some of the names in this book have been changed to protect the privacy of those involved.

Contents

Author's Preface

I am writing this after some time, because I was not ready to do so before. The healing, my own learning and growth, needed to develop to the point where I could be public and open about my awakening and this journey described herein.

Looking back, I see that everything has happened in its own perfect timing as part of the overall plan.

There are many things I could say, but none will take the place of your opening your heart to the pages of this book, and allowing them to inspire and assist you in what is truly the greatest journey imaginable. It is the journey of the self, opening to the true majesty of the self and the wonders of All That Is in the universe.

There is often little scientific proof available to corroborate the truth that is the knowing of the soul, but it is truth nevertheless, and perhaps, even all the more.

Knowing this, you will know that you have been drawn to this book as a soul longing to see more clearly the beauty that is within, and to understand more fully your own Divine connection. I wish you joy in your journey.

Love and Light,

Rosalee Sirgany

From the universal flame of All That Is
To the universal flame here on earth,
Let the light shine freely,
So we may be at one with All That Is.

~ 1 ~

Questioning

And questioning the ideas she learned as a child, she went to the priest, someone who should know spiritual matters. Her concerns were blatantly ignored. The priest seemed so insecure in his own beliefs that he appeared a bit afraid of her questions.

Instead of answering questions about past-life and outer body experiences, he kept clinging to his Bible and saying, "You need to come to church and be rooted in the community. That way your mind won't be taken up with weird imaginings or others' beliefs."

"This is not what others have told me," she said. "These are all things I have experienced, and having experienced them, I know them to be truth."

Again an uneasy look overcame the priest as he said, "You need to come to Church. Do you believe in God? Do you believe in heaven?"

"Yes," she said.

"Then, how can you possibly believe in reincarnation? God made you a special and unique person and if you are to be recycled as another person, then you wouldn't be very unique."

She tried again to make him understand. "The spirit is unique," she said, "and it lives forever. The bodies, or lifetimes, don't detract from that."

"Come to church," he said, completely disregarding her words, "and you will not have these weird thoughts. O.K.?"

"O.K.," she said, finally giving up. "Thanks Father." Then she left, leaving him feeling secure that he had somehow saved her soul from her "own weird imaginings," and yet he had only served to alienate her ever more from the dogma of the religion in which she was raised.

I was the woman in this story and this incident was a turning point in my life. You see, the priest, with all good intentions, wanted me to forget the higher consciousness of which I am aware, that very consciousness that makes me know for certain that God is within me and that I am an intricate part of this universe ~ one with the trees, the sky, the animals and the pure spirit in all mankind.

It is this that he would have me forget in the name of religion.

I cannot forget the knowledge of past-life or past-death experiences that have occurred spontaneously for me in dreams throughout my life, and even more absurdly, why should I ever want to.

That knowledge has led to greater awareness and understanding of who I am now, and that knowledge and oneness with the universe cannot be bought with silver and gold ~ but only through being open to the spirit within ourselves and the people around us.

Isn't that what Jesus taught us ~ to look for the good in people and to do good and be of good heart, mind and spirit toward those around us? Yes, I have found God and I try to be Christ-like every day in my actions.

I have heard that when people seek the truth about historic Jesus, some scholars find that he went traveling alone for several years, during which time he visited the Magi who had visited him at his birth. During this meeting, it is said that the aura surrounding them was so bright, it hurt the eyes to look in their direction.

And I am sure that during his prayers and meditations, Jesus wondered how to enlighten the world with his knowledge of being at one with the universe. He called this reality the Kingdom of Heaven, and it is a place we can all be ~ if we want to find it.

This is the story of my search for the truth, or the many truths, about the universe and our place in it.

***

It had been several years since that day when I had this unusual conversation with the priest and hurried home to write my thoughts about that meeting as well as my reflections on Jesus and his life and my place in the universe.

Then, a short while ago, I found out that many religions, even the Catholic Church, expressed beliefs in reincarnation and past lives in their early writings. These were later removed, mostly for political reasons.

Through the years after these thoughts were written, I continued to get glimpses of other lives and times in my dreams. Then, more recently, amazing coincidences began to happen, and I knew they were not merely chance occurrences at all. I knew there was no such thing as true coincidence and even the most seemingly chance occurrences are for a reason. I realized that everything is part of a plan in some great big overall picture, of which we may only be able to see a small fragment at any given time. It seemed as though I was again at a crossroads, another important turning point in my life.

~ 2 ~

A Beautiful Dream

One day, I awakened remembering a beautiful dream.

I am seated in front of Louise.

Louise is the 74-year old Navajo woman I met while visiting Arizona. It was another of those coincidences that one realizes was not a chance occurrence at all. She came into the coin laundry in Chinle looking almost like a picture post card of an elderly Native American, wearing her brightly colored traditional clothing in shades of purple, red and gold, and sat directly beside me.

We began to talk and she invited my husband, Mike, (now my former husband) and I to her home. It turned out, 48 years ago when Louise was 26, she had the same dream as I about flying over an obelisk. Louise and her family explained that the obelisk is called Spider Rock, and it is said to be the home of Spider Woman, and is one of the holiest of places for Native Americans. It's located in the Canyon de Chelly where they live and where many believe to be the center of the Navajo universe where the web of life interconnects.

I didn't know this when we began searching in Arizona for the red rock obelisk I had flown over like a bird with such a peaceful feeling in my dreams just a few months before our vacation in early November of last year. Louise and her whole family became so very excited after meeting me and hearing about my dream that Louise elatedly told her family she now had *three* daughters, referring to me as her third. There was obviously some sort of cosmic connection, and I was now adopted.

Louise and one of her daughters spent a good part of the next day taking us to Spider Rock and other holy places in the Canyon. They gave me the nickname Birdy Rose, because they sensed I am a "bird spirit," which was apparent to them by my "flying" over Spider Rock in my dream. Before we left, one of Louise's granddaughters gave me a present of two necklaces; one, a string of silver beads with bird fetishes, and the other, a string of red beads interspersed with silver, turquoise and ghost beads (juniper berry seeds). Their friendship made our trip very special.

In last night's dream, Louise is seated facing me, just looking straight ahead. She doesn't say anything. Next to her ~ on her right and in front of me a little toward my left ~ is seated another woman who I get the feeling is somehow related or connected to Louise. I also sense, although I don't actually see, that there is another woman standing between us to my right, just sort of watching or possibly orchestrating all this. We appear to be in a lodge of some kind, as the building is made of logs and there is a log pole behind where they are seated. The four of us complete a circle, with each of us settling in at a point signifying one of the four directions.

The woman who is seated appears to be about Louise's age and I sense that she's Native American as well, but her skin appears lighter, more fair-skinned, as if it were glowing. I can't figure out if she is fair-skinned or if her face is actually glowing! I look at her and I instantly feel so much love from her that although we've never met (that I'm aware of) I have a need to touch her face. I am drawn to her so compellingly.

I reach out my right hand and gently rest my palm on her cheek, which feels smooth, like a young woman's skin. She immediately smiles a beautiful, peaceful smile revealing a perfect set of straight, white teeth. I am completely enraptured by her smile and by the love that I feel, and then I awaken, feeling extremely peaceful, basking in the glow of her love.

Upon awakening, I realized that this was the second time I had this dream. It had come to me once before, within the past couple of days, but I hadn't remembered it. I recall it now, as though it is something very important to remember.

That was the end of January, and I had been trying for months to discover the significance of the dream and who the woman who glowed might be. I met a shaman who said that she was certain the woman was a holy person known to Native Americans as White Buffalo Calf Woman. She appears to Indians at times of need, to bring greater spiritual awareness to the people.

Now I was even more confused. If it was White Buffalo Calf Woman, why would she appear to me and what was I to learn from this meeting? I told Mike, somewhat skeptically, what this shaman had said, but he was concerned that I should be careful about what insights I accepted.

"Why would you have a dream with an Indian holy person?" he asked. "She's probably just a symbolic representation of something. That's how dreams are."

"You're probably right, " I said, "But I really wish I knew what it all means."

It wasn't until about six months later when I was taking a class in Spiritual Awareness, that I would get closer to an answer about the mysteries of this dream. The class was a basic introduction into the spiritual realm and its overview included such topics as how to view auras (the life force energy field that surrounds us all), psychometry (the art of gaining knowledge of a person from a personal possession, usually a piece of jewelry), psychic readings by opening oneself to the aura of another, spiritual healing often called therapeutic touch, and last but certainly not least, an introduction to one of our own guardian angels or spirit guides. The promised meeting with my guide was in fact the real impetus for my taking the course.

I had waited through the twelve long weeks of the course and looked forward to my meeting with great anticipation. When the third of June finally rolled around, I was excited to get to class that evening.

With the help of a medium, I met a guide named Kirstien, who had been my mother in a life in Denmark in the 1890s. Kirstien told me many things that nobody in the class could possibly have known, probably the most significant to me was when she said, "Be assertive, and speak in a voice that can be heard. You have much to offer, Rosalee. Do not hide your light in a corner; let it shine for all to see. And remember that you are never alone. There are many around you who help you."

This was unusual because even though deep down I have always been quite shy, I forced myself to be outgoing. People often commented on how friendly I was. No one understood how I really felt, or so I thought, until Kirstien.

"How can I communicate with you myself?" I asked.

"Just listen," Kirstien replied, "You often hear me now when you are quiet."

I felt a sense of peace having heard that there were many in the spirit realm who help me. Afterward, a couple from the class came up to me and said they saw beautiful auras of spirits circling around me while my guide had been speaking to me through the medium, or channeler, as it is now more commonly called.

"They are in beautiful colors and it looks like there are three or four of them forming a circle around you as if they're protecting you," the wife said as her husband nodded in agreement.

I had not been adept at seeing auras easily, although I could see them when I made a real effort to unfocus my eyes. I didn't quite know what to make of her comment and so I just sort of accepted it for whatever it was worth, along with Kirstien's assurance that there are many around who help me.

At the end of the evening when all students had been given an opportunity to speak for a few minutes with their guide, our instructor suggested that we might try a Ouija board, which he showed us how to use.

"Be careful," he warned. "Don't just ask if any one is there. Ask only for your guides and see what happens."

He also told us that, from his experience, about 95 percent of those who tried would need a partner to work the board, but that some people are able to use the board alone if their energy is strong enough. I didn't give it another thought, but hurried home to tell Mike what my guide Kirstien had said in our meeting.

The following morning I awakened knowing what I had to do. I was so excited I could hardly wait. I was going to the toy store to buy a Ouija board and try it out. "Just maybe, it will work for me," I thought.

I bought a board and tried it immediately, asking for Kirstien to speak with me. To my surprise, the pointer began to move slowly, spelling out words by circling the letters. I followed along expecting it to spell out "Kirstien is here," or something to that effect.

I was certainly surprised when instead the letters spelled out, "Rosalee, no one deserves a baby more than you." I was shocked and amazed all at once. Only someone who knows me intimately would know what that could possibly mean to me. I knew I had connected with my guide and I burst out in tears. It was an inexplicable feeling of being in the presence of someone who you know knows your most innermost thoughts and dreams. After I regained my composure, the board continued to spell out things only someone very close to me would have insights into. Finally I asked with whom I was speaking, and slowly the board spelled out "I am Kirstien." I had connected with my guide in a very precious moment and I was thrilled.

It would only be a short three days later that the energy that wrote its messages across the board would somehow fill me and stir me to open my mouth and speak the messages instead of relying on the board. I had begun to channel, much to my surprise. I could hardly believe it, but when Mike heard me talking in an unusually deep and loud voice, he came in to check on me. "What's going on," he said. The voice stopped and mine took over as I replied, "I do believe I'm channeling." Then I stopped for the evening, feeling exhausted and exhilarated at the same time.

I didn't realize it then, but a whole new world was opening up for me, or maybe I had opened up to it. Either way, it was new to me now, but it was here, and I was going along for the ride, eager to see where it would take me.

~ 3 ~

Spontaneous Regressions

It wasn't long afterward that I began meeting and speaking with more of my guides. There was, in addition to Kirstien, my healing guide whom I had known in Lebanon back in the 1680s when he was my father. He was a physician then, and I, his daughter, studied and followed in his footsteps.

There was also my Indian guide, who had been a great chief of his tribe somewhere in the plains of the Southwestern United States during the time when the white man first arrived to the area. I had been his wife.

It was during my first meeting with Kirstien in the class that I had asked about the woman who glowed in my dreams, convinced now that it must have been a guide who had glowed so beautifully and from whom I had felt such love toward me.

"Are you the woman who glowed in my dreams? " I had asked.

"I think, maybe, I will say yes," was the reply that had been spelled out on the board and uttered by the channeler. Well, that seemed to be a logical explanation with which Mike and I both could be comfortable. I went on each day more and more excited about the things I had been learning from my guides.

I received information about past lives with help from all of my guides. This was geared toward helping me heal past hurts and be able to go forward with my life more settled. There was information on how to create a bright future. And then there were the special dreams that I would learn to understand and fully comprehend the significance of, with the help of Kirstien and my Indian guide, the Chief.

Most often the information came to me in the form of channeled voices which I heard. Other times, the information came through spontaneous regressions when, during my meditations and sometimes in the middle of my channeling, I would suddenly become extremely drowsy. I could hardly keep my eyes open. I knew something unusual was happening, and so I asked the guide with whom I had been working to help take me back to a place I needed to go or to something I needed to see. And then, magically and vividly, as if seeing in a dream, whole scenes of past lives would appear and unfold in front of me.

Once when this occurred I went back to the moment of my death, felt my soul rise as I looked down at my body, that of a young Native American woman dressed in buckskin, and felt myself being engulfed in white light. A voice came, as if from the heavens, which I knew to be one of the Masters. He went over with me all the things I had learned in that life and, when he finished speaking, I was again aware of being back in my room and in this life. It is an awareness I shall never forget.

My days unfolded like this with seemingly small and large miracles, glimpses into the spiritual realm for which I was most grateful.

When I first began channeling on June 6 with the help of the Ouija, I became frustrated at the slow pace at which the information was revealed. A few days later, I asked, "When will I be able to communicate easily and well?" The answer came back, "Give it one moon, give it one moon."

As my guides had promised, it was July 5 and I was now channeling extremely well without the use of the board. This is when I began to explore the very special world of the Dreamtime and my visits to the Lodge.

I asked my guide Kirstien to explain more about the dream with Louise and whether the place we met was some sort of Indian Lodge.

"I am the woman that glowed in your dream and I helped Louise to find you," Kirstien began. "I helped Louise to find you as she had been thinking about you, trying to reach you. She wants to meet with you in the Lodge of Women where you met before. It is a sign that she wants to see you again, Rosalee."

My interest was piqued as Kirstien continued.

"She is waiting for you still. She knows you will come when you can, to visit with her in person. She also looks for you to visit her in spirit, to meet again in the Lodge of Women. It is a place of Indian tradition where women meet to share knowledge and teach one another. It is good to meet her there in spirit whenever you wish. She will know you are there to meet her and she will travel there to meet you in spirit, too.

"That is how it works. Think of meeting with her there and you will be there. You can talk with her there if you wish. You can ask whatever you would like. There are no boundaries of language. You will communicate easily with thoughts, the way you and I and all of us communicate with you and others."

I felt a bit overwhelmed, but Kirstien seemed undaunted by my mood.

"This is how it is. It is just this way. Do not question it. This is how it works and it will be so, if you want to meet her there tonight or any night, just think about your meeting and it will happen," she said.

Then she told me that my Native American guide, the Chief, would like to speak with me. In a few moments, he came through in a deep voice filled with love, which I heard telepathically from somewhere within my being.

"I am glad to speak with you again and glad you wanted to understand more about Louise and your meeting in the Lodge of Women," he began.

"The Lodge of Women is very special indeed. It is where the Dreamers go to speak with one another. It is a place of magic and wisdom. It is a place you have been many times before with the Secret Sisterhood of the Healers. It is a Society of Women who do their healing the natural way ~ with herbs, with will, with energy, with wisdom. This is a Society you have belonged to for hundreds of years, Rosalee. In other lives and times you go back there to your Indian heritage to learn the healing arts.

"In our life together, your Grandma, now Louise, taught you the healing when you were very young. You started as a very young woman and your healing powers were great, renowned, as renowned as your ability to see into the future."

I listened intently as he continued.

"You have repressed this in this life because you have been so hurt for your powers in other lives that deep within, you were afraid. Yet you always wished you could help to heal others by your will, your energy and natural healing herbs. You have felt this need strongly in this life although you have been afraid to voice it."

Knowing there was truth in all he had said about my wanting to help others and wishing I knew how, I continued to listen intently. I felt a bit nervous at the thought of what he was saying, but I was also extremely curious.

"I have heard this in your heart much in this lifetime. Many times you have wished you knew how to help, had the power to help ~ and you do. You can remember what you already know very easily, as easily as you have remembered how to channel our thoughts, and you understand extremely well, my dear Rosalee. Your intuitive ability is remarkable, and you are beginning to realize all this is true.

"You can channel easier each day," the Chief continued, "And you can and will be easily able to heal others and yourself with your will and your knowledge of natural healing. It is your way, and you have done this in many lifetimes."

"Please go back to the Lodge of Women tonight and visit with Louise. She will be waiting there for you, expecting you, and you will learn much from her. Know this. She will be there in the Lodge of Women whenever you visit. Kirstien will help you go if you wish, and you will remember in the morning the things that were discussed and all that you learned. It is good for you to do this and it will help you to help others greatly," he said.

"Now lie down and go to sleep, and as you fall asleep, think of meeting with Louise there and you will visit tonight. You will remember your visit and all you learned in the morning. Do not dwell on the thought of visiting. Just think about meeting there and then release the thought, knowing that a meeting will occur. Do not be afraid. You will enjoy your visit very much and will re-learn much," he continued. "This is good for you. It is your destiny. You will help many in this life with your knowledge, but first you must remember what you know in order to teach, to share, to pass it on.

"Now, just relax thinking of Louise. Kirstien will help see that you get to the Lodge of Women. She is your guide and she will be with you; and remember, my dear, that you have been there often before. Go and remember your knowledge so you can again help. It will be good. You will see.

Your people are in a new age of enlightenment and awareness. They are more open to your knowledge now. Do not be afraid, for you will not be hurt in this lifetime for your knowledge. You will be revered as you were when you were my wife, wife of the Chief of our great Nation, and a great healer and seer in your own right.

"I love you my dear. Good night, sweet dreams and give my love to Louise, please."

I went to sleep following the suggestions of the Chief, not really certain what to expect. To my amazement, the next morning I awakened remembering a Dreamtime visit to the Lodge of Women as vividly as any waking moment.

I am in the Lodge and Louise is there. She is standing with her back toward me about ten feet away. There are crystals of many shapes and sizes hanging on strings from an open beam in the ceiling. She turns to face me and I see that she is looking at the crystals, touching some.

"Crystals are the key to many things," she tells me. "They hold magic. They can heal."

Suddenly, I am lying on a long, narrow table that has very tall legs. Louise is putting stones and crystals all over my body in the area of the chakras. She puts an amethyst on my forehead for the third eye, and sapphire by my throat. She puts emerald on the heart and citrine for yellow near the navel. She puts an orange on my belly for the reproductive chakra and says, "Orange represents the womb of woman, of creativity, like a gourd, but this has more meaning for you since you live in the tropics."

She continues, placing garnet at the base chakra and a darker reddish-pink stone near my ankles on the table.

"The stones are for healing and for balancing," Louise explains. "Stones can heal the body and the spirit. I have taught you this before and now you will remember everything. You were my granddaughter once and my daughter once, and you were a great healer. You still are. You have the knowledge, the power. You will remember everything again. It will all come back to you naturally, and you will heal yourself and others. Feel the energy as you will heal others."

I feel an energy welling up inside me and encircling my entire being.

"This is our way," she tells me. "It is your way and your gift ~ your knowledge for healing. You can heal with crystals and stones and you can also look into a crystal or look into someone's eyes and tell the future."

Then she pauses, and says, "Look around. Look who is here." I look up and greet my dear friend who had passed on about four years ago.

"Marie," I call out, happy to see her.

"It's me, Rosalee," she answers in her slightly British accent. "I'm glad to see you here, glad to be here in the Lodge of Women," she continues. "I am here so that I

can be born as your child. I was Mike's mother once and now I will be his child ~ his child and yours. We are friends across time," she says, referring to the fact that we have known each other in many lives.

"You know this," she says, "And many will recognize me when I am your child. I love you and Mike. Open up and receive me, so that I will be born to you. My name will be Allison Michelle."

And then I suddenly feel my body tremble as her energy merges into mine in the area of my belly. I feel it. It is warm and loving and happy, and I smile as it merges with my energy, with my body. The trembling stops and I relax, feeling peaceful and calm. "I will have a child," I think to myself. I lie there for a moment enjoying the beauty of what has just happened, the miracle of a spirit entering the body to be reborn. Then Louise speaks to me again.

"You are a healer," she says. "Remember what you have learned before. It is there, and will all come back to you. There is no more pain for you in this life. You are free to do your healing and use your psychic powers to help others, and you will be richly rewarded.

"This is your lifetime to enjoy your abilities and reap the harvest you have sown; although these abilities have brought you much pain and sorrow, that is in the past. You will reap rewards now and they are plentiful, my daughter, my granddaughter. We have met here in the Lodge before and will meet here again whenever you wish. I am your teacher through time and I am always here for you."

And then she smiles and looks at me and says, "Go tell the future by looking in people's eyes and hearts, and heal them with your will and your stones and your herbs and your wisdom gathered through time. It is your gift and you have always given it freely, and it has cost you dearly ~

much pain and sorrow ~ but this is no longer. Know you will reap your rewards and all good things will come to you.

"Wear turquoise to open and aid communication," she continues. "Wear silver to be connected with the subconscious, and wear your bird fetishes whenever you wish to travel safely to the Lodge, or whenever you wish. These were given in love and are good luck for you. Wear your ghost beads to help you remember your dreams and the wisdom gained therein. This is good for you. Remember your healing and remember your roots, your heritage. They are good and you are good and wise. You have much knowledge to share about harmony and oneness. Share freely and do not hesitate. This will bring you only just rewards in this life. You will not sorrow.

"Go and heal and see the future and be happy, my child. My prayers go with you, and my strength. We can meet in the Lodge of Women whenever you desire to see me. Now go, Kirstien is waiting."

I went through the day trying to digest and assimilate all I had seen and heard in my Dreamtime meeting in the Lodge. During the afternoon, as I often do, I sat quietly meditating. I was thinking about Marie and how she had visited me during my meditation just a few days earlier. It was my first contact with her, but once I heard her accent and the words she said, I knew who it was.

"The seasons in the sun may be few, but the lessons learned are often many," she had said to me that day. She also told me that she would soon have a very nice surprise to share with me. Now I found myself thinking of last night's Dreamtime visit and Marie's appearance there. "That really was some surprise, Marie," I thought to myself. It all seemed so extraordinary and yet it was so real. Suddenly I heard the words again, and I called out loud, "Marie, is that you?"

"Yes," she said. "It is I, Rosalee, and I know you have many questions about last night and what happened in the Lodge of Women."

"Is it always this way?" I asked through my thoughts. "Is that how spirits become reincarnated?"

"Yes," was Marie's reply. "It is always this way. Once a woman has conceived, the aura around her body drastically changes. It is a sign to those spirits waiting to be born so that they may find an available mother. The aura gets bigger and brighter and remains that way throughout the pregnancy. Now I have entered your womb, merged my energy with yours and this is good. No other spirits waiting to be born may enter now, for they will see you have already been selected as a mother by another soul.

"You see, I may come and go as I wish now," she continued, "entering the womb and leaving at will. This is how it works. Part of my essence will always be with you, however, and others will know they may not enter. This is just the way it works. I will be able to do this, go back and forth at will, until either just before birth or just after birth, whichever I decide. I will be your daughter and Mike's daughter as well, and this is good."

I thanked Marie for explaining all this and went about my day trying to comprehend what had occurred. If I had conceived, it would have been in just the past few days. It all seemed so bizarre, so outside of anything I'd ever experienced that I didn't know what to think, but I could hardly wait for my next visit. That night I went to bed thinking of meeting in the Lodge as I had been told, knowing I was going on a journey into a mystical realm.

~ 4 ~

Gems and Crystals

The next morning I remembered visiting Louise in the Lodge. I hear her say:

"You wear many stones much of the time. They are good for you. You have made wise choices. They help you in ways you do not always understand or realize, but they are good choices for you. Continue to wear whatever stones you feel comfortable wearing, whichever ones you are drawn to wear. Inside your heart, you know which ones are for you."

There is a sparkle of love in her eyes as she looks into mine. She is sitting across from me in the same place as my first dream with Louise, and she is smiling now with a wonderful twinkle in her eyes.

"It will all come back to you," she continues. "It is coming back now more everyday. Do not rush it. The knowledge, the ability are yours. It cannot be taken from you. Do not worry, it will all come back to you soon. It is just this way. The knowledge is yours; it is just a little

hidden from you at the moment. You are a powerful seer and healer and this will all return soon ~ all your abilities and strengths. It is just the way it is my granddaughter, my daughter, my dear friend and student through time. You have journeyed much to find your way, and you will remember everything. It is this way. It is how it is. Go now and rest, for you need your energy. I am glad you are visiting and remembering your heritage and your abilities. Grandma loves you. Now go, Rosalee, and get some sleep. I love you through time and space. Now rest."

As I recalled my Dreamtime conversation, I realized that I had awakened still somewhat tired, as though my Dreamtime visit had intruded into my usual hours of sleep.

I continued going about my days with my usual routine, which now also included channeling one or more of my guides. A few days later my Native American guide suggested that I visit again in the Lodge of Women. That night, I knew I was going on a journey ~ traveling to the mysterious land of the Dreamers. I awakened again with the distinct feeling that I had been to the Lodge.

After I straightened up the house that morning, I sat quietly meditating and tried to remember my Dreamtime experience. In a few moments the picture came to life.

I see Louise greeting me.

"Hello, my daughter, my granddaughter, my student and friend across time. I am glad you have visited this evening. Did the Chief tell you I have been longing to visit with you again here in the Lodge of Women?" she asks.

I nod yes silently, and notice she has something in her hands.

"My dear, I have much to show you tonight," Louise is saying. She is standing near the center of the wooden Lodge, about ten feet away from me, holding a mortar and pestle in her hands.

She is crushing something in the bowl.

I am suddenly standing directly in front of her, only about a foot away. Louise looks deep into my eyes.

"You are a visionary, a great seer," she says. "It has always been this way with you.

"I have crushed the stones for you, the ones you need ~ crystal and tourmaline ~ crystal for clarity of thought and tourmaline for clarity of vision."

I notice that the mortar is no longer in her hand. It has disappeared. She holds the medicine bowl close to her heart with her left hand and plays with some residue from the mixture, rubbing it between her fingers. Then she takes her right thumb and smudges it again into the crushed mixture in the medicine bowl. She again rubs her thumb and forefinger together with the mixture she has gotten from the bowl and touches my forehead, smudging the mixture in the area of the third eye.

"Now your vision and your mind will always be very sharp and clear and vivid," she says, as she wipes the area a couple of times before moving her thumb to my left eyelid, which closes as her finger approaches my eye. She strokes her thumb gently across my left eyelid and then wipes some of the crushed residue on my right eyelid, and then on the area of the third eye again, right between the two eyebrows, and across my forehead.

Then she gazes into my eyes again, with the most loving, sincere look in her eyes and I realize that I am feeling very comfortable and at peace with myself and all that is happening.

"Know this," she says. "You can always rely on your visions and your knowing. They are good and will help you in many ways that you do not always understand and comprehend, my daughter, but they are reliable nevertheless. Know you can always count on what you see

and feel. They are very real, your gifts of insight and intuition, and should not be ignored.

"I want you to always see with clarity of vision, my child. You have always done this in many lifetimes and in the present lifetime this gift is returning rapidly to you because you have learned once again, although much later than usual for you, how to open up to it. Your visual nature is returning, and this will ensure clarity of that gift of vision for you. The tourmaline and crystal will make your mind always sharp and clear, for you will need it to see those around you from a clear perspective. Their motives and intentions will be clear.

"If you feel and see someone's intentions are not good, pure, tell them you will not be able to read for them. It's as simple as that. You will know even from their voices. You will just know, and for those, you will tell them you will not be able to read for them. Tell them you do not always read for anyone, but if they would like to try another time, you will see if you will be able to read.

"As the Chief related to you very well last night, when you read for others, it is your obligation and responsibility to tell them what you see. They have come to you for a reason and the reason may be so that they will be warned to modify their actions to change their destiny. The Chief could advise you well in this area because he has heard you give news that has been frightening or unpleasant many times."

She stares into my eyes with her shining eyes, giving me a gentle smile.

"The Chief has been with you in many lifetimes and has learned much from you, and from the way you give unpleasant news to people. He has watched and heard you do this. I have been there too, as your teacher, and I have seen much also, which right now you may not even believe

you are capable of. But for now, suffice it to say that what the Chief has told you is always the best way. Be open and honest at all times when you read for others, even though what you are seeing, feeling or picking up may be frightening or unpleasant. Preface your comments lovingly and gently, breaking it to them slowly.

"Remember, it is the person's choice whether to act on what you have told them. They may not wish to change their destinies or those of the people around them. Destiny is always a personal choice, and you must respect their choice.

"Your only responsibility is to pass on the messages you receive so the people will have an opportunity to change their destinies if they wish. You are only providing a warning. They may decide to do nothing to change their destiny. You see, they may not believe you are right. This is the case sometimes, when disturbing visions are seen, but know you have fulfilled your responsibility by telling them what you have seen and breaking it to them gently.

"The visions that you may see of a disturbing nature may not always come to pass. There may be others involved who may do something, changing the destiny you have seen. Do you understand? Nothing is guaranteed and even the most vivid vision may or may not come to pass depending on the many events and people that are involved."

"Yes, Grandma," I say, nodding.

"Either way, by passing along what you have seen or felt, my child, your part has been done," she continues. "Your responsibility is over. We all must accept responsibility for our own lives, and even our own death. We decide, and you know this. It is something you have always known.

"This is all I wanted to share with you, and I am thankful that the Chief gave you my message. I am pleased, my child. Now return to your bed and your dreams and your husband and your world and remember me often. Remember also, whenever you wish to talk with me we can visit here in the Lodge of Women," she says.

"Now, go and wake in your bed and know you can rely on your vision and on your intuition to light your path as you travel this new journey on the Good Red Road.

"Know that I am with you always, watching over you and guiding you, and I will be here whenever you wish to visit with me again in the Lodge of Women. Now go, for it is getting rather late and you need your rest."

The scene disappears to my awakening in my bedroom, the morning light peeking through the blinds.

During the next two weeks, I spent much time channeling my guides and had begun to learn and understand more about my past lives.

One day, with the help of my healing guide, I started gaining insight into why I had experienced some minor back and neck pain from time to time. As appeared to be quite common with me, these had their roots in another life and time. These insights seemed to be helping because, knowing what the cause was, I began to adjust my lifestyle and my thinking in order to eliminate, or at least alleviate, these symptoms.

I had also begun getting some terrible headaches that would ease for a few short hours, or for a day, and then return. My healing guide explained that these headaches were due, in large part, he said, "to the fact that you are afraid to confront your psychic abilities with regard to your visions and intuition."

Although I was excited about everything I was learning, I also realized that I was starting to feel quite tired a lot of the time. I wondered if the psychic activity was taking a toll on my body.

I found myself in the Lodge of Women visiting with Louise.

"Now, you need to relax also," she starts to say. "You need to settle down and understand your true self and your place in the scheme of things, and I will help you.

"Listen to your body and your heart. Learn this and you will have learned much, my child. I want you to remember something. I am with you always and I will be here for you whenever you wish to visit and learn. It is the way we share our knowledge; the Dreamers bring us together in the Lodge of Women to learn and to share knowledge and experience so we can become enlightened and empowered within our own beings. It is a gift we share with the Dreamers and our ancestors, and it is a very good gift, my daughter.

"A wise man once told you that you would be a great seer in this life," she continues, "a woman of great psychic abilities and healing powers. He gave you a jade and a rose quartz. The jade, he said, was for money, and the rose quartz was for love. You have these stones still, put away, and now you must find them and take them with you whenever you visit friends from the other side, other dimensions."

I wonder how she knows about the man that I had met one afternoon and what he had said and his gift of little smooth tumbled stones, one each of pink and green, which he had given me for good luck, but I am distracted from my thoughts again by Louise.

"In your heart, take these stones with you, and you will begin to understand all that you see. All that is taught will be much clearer to you. You see, the jade brings wisdom and knowledge and the rose quartz brings

emotional peace and security, and these are what you need now. You have a jade and rose quartz in your pouch already," she says, referring to the pouch I often carry in my pocket with some special stones I have gathered through the years.

"This is good that you carry these. Remember his gift of jade and rose quartz when you travel and it will bring you closer to a clearer understanding. These stones from him were a gift given in pure love and his intentions were all good. His intentions made these stones very powerful for you and this is why you must try to locate them now physically.

"They will help you tremendously, my daughter, in your seeing. Your psychic visions and powers of healing will be greatly improved, and they are already superior among psychics and healers. Remember no one can stop the forces that are behind you, driving you to show and help others with your powers, for you are driven by the power of love, and love is the greatest power there is. You truly love mankind and wish to help each and every person," Louise says, gazing into my eyes.

"This is what has made your abilities so strong for so many lifetimes; your ability to love, and it is exceeded by your ability to share your gifts and abilities with others. You are a great visionary of our time, a great healer too, and you will come to recognize this very soon."

For a moment I find myself with a feeling of terror, a fear which has gripped me from a deep, emotional level at the heart of my being upon hearing her words. Again, she interrupts my panic.

"For now, please do not be afraid of your visions or your knowing and be confident. They are extremely accurate. It has always been this way with you and this time is no different.

"You are wondering why you're such a late bloomer in this life, and now you know in your mind and heart that you had repressed your abilities and your vast knowledge out of fear. A very real fear when you consider what you have endured and how you have suffered and been killed many times in the white man's world for your knowledge and abilities."

I am overcome by fear as she speaks, so powerful is the feeling, that I feel I will burst into tears, but Louise continues.

"But this time it is different. The new age of enlightenment is here, Rosalee, and people hunger and thirst for the knowledge and wisdom you have bottled up all your life. It is coming forth now like the gushing of the river, a river whose flow cannot be dammed up."

Again, a feeling of sheer terror courses through my body as I feel the area of my solar plexus become very tense and it seems every muscle in my body begins to tighten with inexplicable fear. Just then, Louise again stirs me back to her presence with a soft, clear voice.

"You see what is happening in the Midwest," she says, referring to the flooding taking place there. "No one can stop the river's natural flow, and it is a message not to even try. And the river that is your knowledge and ability must be allowed to flow freely. It must be allowed to overflow onto the banks, which is the multitude, the masses of people who will benefit by your abilities and knowledge. You cannot dam up the river successfully, nor can you dam up or hide away your abilities as a visionary and healer.

"These are your gifts to share with the world, my child," she says lovingly. "They should be shared freely and without hesitation. I know you understand what I say. That is good," she says, looking at me with a smile.

"I will let you get your rest now. Go back home to your bed, as you need your rest. We can meet here again whenever you wish. Go now, my child, before it is much later and we will spend too long. Go now, and remember I am here whenever you wish to visit and learn and grow. I am with you always."

"Yes, I know," I say. "It's good to be able to visit you whenever I feel the need to do so. I'm so glad I understand how to visit and share knowledge again. I will not be afraid. You will see. It will be all right for me now. I am going to be fine."

I feel like I am really trying to convince myself.

She looks at me and smiles. "Yes," she says, "I know you are, my granddaughter, my daughter, my student and friend across time. You will be just fine. I am pleased. And now you must go, but we will visit again soon. Whenever you are ready, just think of me and I will meet you here and we can talk and share some more. I always enjoy you and I am pleased, my daughter. Now, go."

The scene disappears and I am back in my bedroom, waking to the remembrances of Dreamtime travel to the Lodge of Women.

I went through my day, trying to assimilate all I had heard in the Lodge, and felt a bit more at ease and peaceful as the day progressed.

Although I was still quite tired, my thirst for knowledge brought me again to a meeting in the Lodge just a couple of nights later.

I am standing in the Lodge and Louise has her back toward me. She turns around to face me and begins to speak.

"Rosalee, I am glad you have visited with me this evening even though you are very tired. I have much knowledge to share with you about your body and your

health, much that will help you a great deal. Tremendous knowledge is yours for the asking, and now I will share the secret to good health for you. You have overcome the worst already in your life. You have faced your past-life traumas and have let go the fears and the pain and this is good, but still, you must know certain things to be perfectly and completely healthy.

"Be aware that water is the most important thing for your body. It is in your body. The body is made up largely of water and this is your body's river, the river that keeps the body supple and healthy just as the river does with the land.

"Your body is plagued with scar tissue from much surgery. If you have pain on your left side it is the scar tissue acting up, and the main cause of this is mild dehydration due to not enough fluids in your diet. You need to drink plenty of water, my daughter, and it will keep you young and healthy.

"Also, be mindful of what you eat. I am aware you like natural foods without chemicals and preservatives. This is good for you, as you know. Do not sway from this. It is better to drink water or juice or healthy liquids than to put chemicals in your body. The chemicals block the natural vitamins in the food from being absorbed by the body. Eat regularly and try not to wait long if you are hungry. Enjoy even a little light snack as soon as you can when you get hungry.

"Remember, also, that if you feel pain in the left side, drink extra water and fluids for the next few days and you will feel much better. Just be mindful to eat often and well ~ natural, healthy foods ~ and drink plenty of water. It is good for you, my dear," she says, and stares into my eyes with a strong, fixed gaze.

I was about to ask how she knew all these things about me and, just then, she slaps her hands on her thighs and says, "Now I will tell you a story of how I know so much about you and the things happening to you."

I look at her, longing for the answer and wondering how she knows exactly what I am thinking, when she begins to speak.

"I am your teacher and friend across time, Rosalee, and we have shared many lives together as student and teacher. It is this that brings us together now, my daughter. You are my student again. The Indian ways, ways of the spirit, allow me to think about you and know exactly what you are going through, what is happening with you and around you at any given time. My powers are not so great, given that I have been doing this over so many lifetimes, and with you it is very easy because we are so close; in spirit we are always close, almost inseparable.

"I am your teacher over time and you are my student, and we have traveled many lifetimes together and always we are teacher and student," she continues. "It is my job to help you find your full potential, to be all you can be for yourself and all those around you. It is a good and worthy purpose. Your life's work is to share knowledge with many and this you will do, my daughter," and she gazes into my eyes with a twinkle, a knowing sparkle in her eyes that seems warmed by the wood of the Lodge.

"You will do this well, but first you must retrieve the knowledge you have had in the past and have forgotten."

I listen intently as she continues.

"As I have said, much of this knowledge was repressed by you because of the pain you have suffered, and now you have let go of the pain and suffering of your past lives and are ready to make headway with your life's purpose in this life. This could not be done any sooner, not

before you let go the hurts of the past and freely accepted and came to terms with your abilities, my dear."

I look at her wanting to believe I have let go of all my fears but something deep inside still haunts me ~ a fear I cannot explain. Louise interrupts my thoughts, as though she is reading my mind again.

"But you have let go," she says in a full and loving voice, "and now you are regaining your ancient knowledge, and this will help many. You are a natural writer and your work is very good. Many will be enlightened by your writing. In this new age you are totally safe. Men and women will again revere you for your abilities, for they will see your closeness to the spirit world, to All That Is. It is good, my child, and I am glad to be your teacher once again.

"In your terms, it is almost as though we are twins. We are on the same wavelength, so to speak," and she smiles. "I know you understand this term and now I think you have a clearer understanding. Please remember. Do not fight the urge to visit in the Lodge of Women even when you are tired, except if the physical reason is of the utmost importance. Otherwise, spirit always knows best, so just let go and come and visit here in the Lodge. Now, it is time for your return to the land of the physical, and you will remember this when you awaken."

Then I awakened in my bed. It was 4 a.m., and I knew I had visited Louise in the Lodge of Women.

~ 5 ~

The Book of Knowledge

About two weeks went by before I had another Dreamtime visit. I awakened at 2:30 a.m. knowing I had again been to the Lodge of Women. I went back to sleep and in the morning light remembered seeing Grandma in the Lodge.

"My child, I am glad you are here," she says. "There is much for you to learn. I am trying to teach you as much as possible in as little time as possible. You are relearning what you already know and this is why your learning can be so quick. You are re-learning, and this is easy.

"I have something to show you," she says, holding something in her outstretched hands. "It is a book of knowledge," she explains. "It is many centuries old and its pages hold much you already know. There is much still to learn my child, and we are learning together in a way, even though you are the student and I am the teacher. I am the catalyst for your learning and you for mine. It is said

teachers learn from their students and I am learning from you as much as you are learning from me. It is how it is. It is the way of knowledge.

"Now, let us begin. I am here with you this morning to share knowledge of the future, how it is manifested and how it can be created and changed to your liking. I am sure you are already familiar with this concept. We create our own realities. I am talking of a new house, for example, or whatever you want. You must draw this reality into being for yourself and Mike and you can do this in many ways, my dear."

She looks into my eyes with a sparkle, a twinkle in her eyes, the light of wisdom glowing from deep within.

"I am your teacher. Let me explain how this works. We are here together because we have wanted it this way. We have been drawn together in the land of the Dreamers because we wanted to meet here to learn and to share knowledge, and to grow as we have done so often, in so many lifetimes. I am here because I want to be here with you. You have drawn me here and I have drawn you. Do you understand, my child? Are you following this concept?"

"Yes Grandma, I understand."

"Well, then, it is the same way with everything in life. We draw to us what we want in our lives. You have drawn your abilities and your psychic and healing powers to you many times in many lifetimes because you saw a need to help others naturally and sought the way to do this yourself. Your psychic and healing abilities are a result of your desire to help others naturally, without artificial means.

"You can forewarn people of impending disaster or disturbing news, offering a chance for them to change the destiny they have already chosen. You offer hope to those

in despair or longing for friendship when you can read their future and see positive and happy events and times for them. You give them hope, you uplift their present life so they carry on, happy in the hope that what you have seen is correct and their future will be happier and better than the present."

I begin thinking to myself that although I've had some extraordinary spiritual experiences, I have never thought of myself as having any special psychic abilities. I've taken my Spiritual Awareness class and learned how to develop my psychic abilities, but I realize everyone can learn these abilities as long as they are open to all the possibilities of the universe. Louise interrupts my thoughts.

"You have drawn your abilities from your need and desire to help all mankind and especially those around you, and you have always been able to find strength in this.

"You can communicate telepathically with others regardless of the miles between the physical bodies. Telepathy is that way. You can communicate instantly as though you were together in the same room. I know you understand this well. It is the basis for your psychic powers, your ability to tune in to others even when they are at a distance, and you do this well."

Again I can feel my mind starting to protest these abilities and again Louise's voice brings me back to what she is saying.

She looks deep into my eyes again and says, "So it is with anything you want. You have started the balls rolling, so to speak, and they are rolling your way. Everything is in your court, and you can make things happen now just the way you want them to.

"For instance," she continues, "If you want to pay a certain price for a particular house, just think of it and it

will be so. If you wish to be moved in by a certain date, just envision and imagine it and this will come true.

"We create our own realities, Rosalee, and you already know this. It is most important. Do not forget this rule. We create our own realities. Your life is working out for you just as you have wished and you will have everything you want in life. You have been told this often by many who are perceptive and wise, and it is so. You are creating for your life what you want by your positive outlook and this is translated to your physical being, your physical life and surroundings.

"Now let us take a walk outside in the woods. It is nice outside and we can talk as we walk."

Instantly, we are in the woods just outside the Lodge and we are walking barefooted among the Ponderosa pines and the sagebrush, and Louise says, "We have lived many times together in the woods among the trees and it has taught us much, the woods.

"In nature is everything we humans need to learn, and all the species here will teach us when we are open to the teachings of the universe. It is how it is. It has always been this way. We are one with the sky beings and the creature beings, the four-legged and winged ones. We are one with All That Is, and you know this and remember it well my daughter, but you do not always take time to be with nature and this is something you need more of.

"When you were Hiawatha and I was your grandmother, we walked often in the woods and saw many things, many wondrous things. You used to come into the woods by yourself to pray and to think and to just be alone with yourself and the splendor of All That Is. It is good for you to do this, Rosalee. It puts you in touch with your true being, your inner self, that part of you that is all knowing,

that part in each of us we can all touch if we know how ~ and you know how very well my daughter.

"Now it is time to regain your knowledge that comes from being one with nature and with the universe. You already have this to some extent, but to really, truly walk in beauty you must learn again how the animals interact with one another and with man. To do this you should find yourself a place in the woods. It does not need to be a dense forest as long as it is wooded and natural enough to make you feel comfortable and totally at peace, at one with nature and with yourself.

"The important thing is to find a spot that appeals to you and just relax there, contemplating, watching, waiting, seeing what goes on all around you. See the beauty and majesty of All That Is and know that you are one with the universe, and all the creatures who attract your attention have done so in order to share with you their own special knowledge and gifts.

"Watch them carefully," she continues. "Their behavior will tell you much. It will be a lesson or a message for you and you will understand what that is if you have been sitting quietly. You will understand their messages and they will always help you. It is how it is. We Indians have always known this, and you know it too. Just wait and watch and listen and you will learn all you need to learn about yourself and about others ~ how you interact with them and they with you. The animals are great teachers. Watch and learn my daughter. Learn the knowledge you have forgotten."

As we continue to walk I notice the beauty of the pines overhead and the earthy smell of the forest.

"Go out into your garden and learn," Louise says, "and I will be here whenever you wish to return to the Lodge. We can meet and talk again. I am pleased my dear

Birdy Rose, that we can talk as we do and share our thoughts so freely. We have done this many times and this is no different. Now go, before it gets too late. I will see you again very, very soon."

Not a moment later, I was awake in my bed and glanced over at the clock. It was 2:30 in the morning and I knew another Dreamtime visit had been completed.

The next day I went out into my garden. The pale blue afternoon sky was overcast and the gentle breeze felt pleasant as it caressed my face. I sat there for a while just being quiet looking at the things that caught my attention as Louise had instructed in the Dreamtime. As she had said, the messages became very clear.

I noticed the flow of the water in the canal and realized it was teaching me to flow like water with the ever-changing currents and winds, to go with the flow and know all things work out as they should.

I noticed the bumble bee dancing from flower to flower and I sensed it was telling me to pollinate or sow the seeds of my gifts and abilities, to share my talents with many with whom I might come in contact.

The coconut palms gently swaying in the breeze taught me to be like the palms, to sway with the winds but gently keep my center, just as the trunk is the center, and the fronds reach far to form a well balanced tree. It sways and sways but keeps its center, its balance. Even through the worst of storms nothing takes it off its peaceful, gentle center for too long. I should be like the palm trees I admire so often for the peaceful feeling they create, I thought.

The birds singing merrily along their way are teaching me to enjoy life as I go along, to express myself, let my spirit soar and be happy.

The brightly colored butterflies gently floating from one small red jatropha flower to the next teach me to touch the lives of others with gentleness and beauty and to be light-hearted that I may gently float above the madness.

The lizard is unperturbed by the bumblebees or others in its path. It lets nothing keep it from its task of finding food, and teaches us to let nothing keep us from our goals, our path in life.

Feeling totally peaceful and at one with the universe, I stayed there for quite a while before going back inside to write in my journal all that nature had taught me.

I went about my days after that with my usual routine of our landscape design business a little more mindful of the true messages in nature around us.

During this time I met another of my guides, whose name was Heidi. She told me she had been my guide before in another life. I continued to channel information from my guides about other lives and things that were pertinent to me. Occasionally I would go into regressions with the help of my guides so I would have a glimpse of a former life, which I needed to see in order to gain perspective and understanding.

It was also at about this time that I began channeling for others, introducing them to their own guides. I received a wonderful new prayer for channeling from Heidi, which she said was not new at all, but one which I had given others in another life:

Please help me be one with the light,
And my guides as well,
That they may guide me well,
And I may also guide others as well.

During the days that followed, I was beginning to wonder if the Lodge of Women and all I have seen take place in my travels there were real, or were they just figments of my imagination. Heidi assured me that the Lodge is very real, indeed, and that all the fascinating things that I have seen and experienced there are all very real as well.

One week passed before I again met with Louise in the Lodge of Women.

"My daughter, I am glad you have come to me this early morning," Louise says. "Let us take another walk in the woods and we can talk as we have before. You can tell me of your quiet time in your garden and all that you learned there, my child."

Suddenly, we are again walking in the woods. The moonlight is friendly, lighting our path just enough to see and walk comfortably through the pines and the sage and other under-brush, bushes with berries, and pine needles beneath our feet. The air smells clean and fresh.

"It is good to take a walk in the woods," she says. "They are a quiet place for meditation and contemplation and this gives one a fresh, new perspective of all they have been going through." Then she turns toward me, and adds, "And all you have been going through." I know she is referring to the confusion I have been having regarding some personal matters.

"It is for a reason," she continues. "For your knowledge and growth, my child. It is the reason for everything. All of this is merely an illusion to help us fulfill what we need in order that we may learn and grow in love, in understanding, in caring and in forgiving. Forgiving ourselves as well as others is sometimes the most difficult lesson to learn and you are learning this now.

"You have learned this lesson well and now you need to let go and be able to trust again. It is not easy my dear after all you have been through, but you must trust in the goodness, the light of All That Is in the universe.

"You remember this well from your days as a spirit woman who helped the Indians in their time of need. You were White Star Woman and appeared to many in their times of need. You brought advice and hope. Hope to allow them to hold on for better times, a better life, and to remember their oneness with the light; to remind them to walk in the light. And this is good for you to remember now, my dear daughter.

"I want you to remember this now. Always look to walk in the light and be one with the light and all good things will light your path. You will walk in beauty, as we Indians say, on this earth walk. You will walk in the light, share your light for others to see. It is brilliant as it was when you were White Star Woman."

My mind wanders as I remember that I've heard this from Heidi, but somehow the idea that I have been a spirit woman in a past life is just a little too far-fetched for me to accept as reality. Louise interrupts my thoughts.

"At that time, Heidi was your guide, as she has told you, and you were not so sure if you should believe. But you will learn that you can trust again and especially that you can trust Heidi.

"She was your guide when you were White Star Woman, as she said, and she has been with you many times in many lifetimes when you have been at your spiritual best ~ when your sense of oneness was keenest and strongest. This is again opening up for you. Heidi understands your deepest fears and concerns and will guide you well my child, as she has always. This will be a very good time for you ~ a time of oneness ~ and it will be a fruitful and productive time for you spiritually and physically."

Louise stops and turns to look at me directly for a moment.

"This is your time, and you will fulfill your goals," she says. "You will write, my child, and share your knowledge with many, and this is good because you have much to give, much knowledge to share, and I am pleased and happy that you will be sharing this with so many in this life.

"You know this is your purpose, your goal in this lifetime, and you will accomplish this, and it will be very well received, my dear."

We start walking again as she continues.

"You will know what format to use. It will come to you, but for now, do not rush that part, for you are learning much that will be helpful to pass along in your writing, and your time is being taken up with this relearning now.

"It is good and necessary. When you feel like writing, write, and it will come as a flow, as it does for you. You will all of a sudden simply know how it should be put together, and it will work very well for you. You will see. Others will help you disseminate your message of knowledge and harmony and oneness."

I listen carefully, wanting to believe all that she is saying.

"Others in both dimensions will help you in these endeavors as they have before and as you have helped others before, my dear," she says, and looks at me with that loving twinkle in her eyes.

"Kirstien was right when she told you of others who would open doors for you, your work," she continues. "And the Chief was correct when he told you that your books will be read by millions. It is meant to be this way. Your knowledge is meant to be shared with so many ~ and you will do this my daughter, and very well indeed."

We walk along in the woods for a while and then Louise says, "Now let us come sit by the bank of the river and talk some more. I want to hear all about what you learned in your visit to your garden. Tell me my child."

As suddenly as she says this, we are sitting on a large rock on the bank of a river that flows gently behind us as we speak. The sound of the water makes everything feel even more peaceful as I begin to speak. I tell her of the palm trees that never get off their center, no matter what.

"That is important," she says. "You must learn to stay in your center no matter what storms are going on around you. And what else did you learn?" she asks, resting her palms just above her knees as she looks at me with a pleased, little smile, a knowing smile.

"I learned from the bumble bees, not just to take but to give back of myself, my knowledge, to all with whom I come in contact."

"Good, and what else?"

"I learned from the flow of the water in the canal, to flow with the tides, to be flexible in my mind and attitudes and feelings ~ to be flexible enough to learn new things, new ideas and to be able to grow."

"Good, my child," Louise says, this time with a bigger smile that somehow lights up her entire face. "What else did you learn?"

"The lizard keeps focused on his task no matter what obstacles are in his path. I need to do that, too. And the butterfly flits and floats beautifully from flower to flower collecting nectar no matter what confusion is around, what noises are there. It floats quietly and gently and this teaches me to float quietly above the madness that sometimes exists, to walk in beauty and in peace and harmony with myself and the rhythm of the universe," and I look at her and smile.

"You have done well, my daughter. You have learned much and I am very pleased. I am glad you are

learning so well. You will be ready to begin your life's work rather soon I feel, very, very soon indeed, and it will be good and you will be successful.

"Do not fear, for everything will work out as it should. As you know, things always do. I am proud of you my dear, as you are learning very well and quickly, and I am pleased.

"Now you must go. It is time for you to get back in your bed and rest, for you will need it for the journeys that are ahead of us."

"Thank you Grandma," I say, hugging her closely. "I feel so much better. I am learning much and understand so much more. I feel better about everything ~ myself, my guides, the whole world, the universe ~ everything seems to be in a better perspective, more ordered somehow. I feel better about my place in this ordered reality, the order of things. It is good. I feel so much better."

"I will see you again very, very soon," Louise says, smiling at me. Then she pats my knees, and we are no longer there.

The next thing I know is that I am awakening in my bedroom and that another Dreamtime visit has taken place.

~ 6 ~

Ancient Healing Arts

About ten days later I awoke at 1:17 a.m. with a terrible headache and severe stomach cramps. After a while I realized I had visited the Lodge of Women. Heidi agreed. She said that if I got out of bed and remembered my visit, my pain would go away.

I got out of bed with my journal and pen in hand and went into the living room. As I began to write, the whole picture of my Dreamtime visit with Louise began to replay before my eyes.

"I am glad you have come my dear daughter, my Birdy Rose. I have wanted to talk with you many times when you were menstruating and in pain, but your pain has kept you from the Lodge, my dear, when this is the very place you needed to be.

"I am glad you have come now. We have much to discuss. I am your mother, grandmother, your friend and teacher over time and I am glad you have come tonight for there is much to share in order for you to grow and really release this pain you have been dealing with for so long.

Since you began menstruating in this life, your pain has been great and it distresses you.

"You thought this would stop, for you have been told your healing is completed," she says. I realize that she is referring to the past-life regression work I had been doing, not only with a prominent psychiatrist famous for his work in this field, but also with my own healing guide who was trying to help me get over my past-life hurts.

"You are a spirit, however," she says, as she gazes into my eyes, continuing. "And a healer in our Indian traditions. This Lodge of Women, this place of spirit, has brought you to me many times over many lifetimes. You are to be the healer you are now, and have been over many lifetimes. Tonight, in this Lodge of Women, you will learn to heal yourself just as you have done before as a spirit woman in this Lodge.

"You are a part of a secret society known as the Society of Women Healers and as I have told you before, your healing ability is great and beyond the belief and understanding of many. It is this you will re-learn tonight ~ and learn you will ~ how to help yourself and others."

I look into her eyes and she looks into mine.

"We will begin at a point you already know," she says. "The chakras. These chakras must be aligned for the body to be in proper working order. It is not the only necessary requirement, however.

"Now, you have seen how you can balance the chakras with many colored stones. You also use your helper crystal for balancing your chakras, and this is good," she says. I know she is referring to the quartz crystal pendulum I sometimes use to balance my chakras when I meditate.

"You understand this well," she continues. "The pressure points throughout the body are important to you

as well. In your body, they will signal you, speak to you as it were, by giving you or sending you a tingly or itchy sensation in the area or areas of the body that need help.

"Then there is the aura to be treated. To clear blocked energies and repair any holes and gaps is important. Do this by envisioning a cocoon or halo of white light around you or the person to be healed. Then examine this halo closely. Are there any holes, any gaps upon close inspection? You will always see the hole or feel it if there is one, and you will know where it is.

"You will stop now and do this for yourself when you remember this visit to the Lodge and reach this point in our conversation. Please stop and do this healing for yourself then ~ and you will need to connect with your higher self when you do this."

I stopped recalling my Dreamtime visit and did as I was requested. I envisioned myself for what felt like hours, wrapping myself in a cocoon of white, healing light ~ the light from the love of God ~ pure energy being drawn in from the universe.

First, I plugged holes in front of my heart, in front and back of my neck, in the middle of my back, and the solar plexus area. A rather big hole went from my heart and extended straight down through the solar plexus area and into the stomach. It took much time to plug.

Next, I carried the cocoon of light around my head and torso and down both sides of my hips to my thighs. Then, finally, I quickly wrapped a halo of light around my legs and feet, and then re-wrapped the halo around my entire body again and again, filling holes, making sure to complete the halo of light.

After that I started to breathe deeply and a recollection of the Dreamtime visit came back to me as I heard Louise.

"Then you will breathe deeply, at least four deep and cleansing breaths," she is saying. "Breathe in through your nose and expand the stomach first and then the chest. Let it fill completely, then gush it out through your mouth.

"Relax and let it all happen. You will fall asleep and you will dream a healing dream. This will be shared with others and it will complete your healing my dear Hiawatha, my dear Birdy Rose," she said, "and I will see you again next when you wish to visit.

"Now, after you remember your visit and heal yourself and your aura, and have your healing dream, my dear, you will once and forever be completely and perfectly well. I thank you for visiting tonight. The courage was great as you did not feel well at all and it takes courage to travel willingly in spirit when one is not well.

"Now, go and heal yourself, and I will see you when you are perfectly well and you will have pain no more. Now, go my child and be healed and be well," and she looks at me with a smile as she touches my shoulder and brushes back my hair. Then she looks, actually gazes, into my eyes, her eyes twinkling as she says again, "Be well my dear, sweet friend, my daughter. I am pleased you will be all and completely well very soon indeed.

"I am happy for you my child; and remember to write down your healing dream and share it with many. It is in the sharing of this dream that the healing will be secured. Rest assured, you will be better, and I do mean all better, completely healed and free of these pains and all and any pains you have suffered in this and past lives.

"You will be completely well and you will then be able to heal others with extreme proficiency. Now go," she says, as she puts her hand on my shoulder, "and perform your healing well, my dear. I am so pleased. I will see you again soon."

Then I awakened. It was already 3:45 by the time I had finished recalling this Dreamtime visit, performing my healing, and was getting back into bed.

When I awakened with the morning light I remembered my healing dream.

I am in a small boat, a canoe with high sides. I am on a lake and the water is perfectly still, like glass, except for the tiny ripples circling out from my boat.

A brown swan comes alongside the boat and stops. He looks as if he's greeting me, so I say "Hello, and how are you?" He seems to smile back a greeting and from somewhere, telepathically, or I don't know where, he says,

"In harmony is the key to all healing."

"Harmony?" I ask.

"Yes," he replies. "Harmony is the key to all healing. When you are in harmony within and without, you will be well. Without perfect harmony, you cannot be totally well. Herein lies the key to health. It is harmony within the self and different aspects of the self, and harmony with the environment and all that is around you that will make you well.

"And inner peace comes from harmony," he continues, "And also brings greater harmony. Find inner peace and you will find harmony and you will be well."

And with that he swims off, creating the tiniest ripple of a V behind him in the water of the tree-lined lake.

Later that day I communicated at length with my healing guide. He explained more about why I was still experiencing pain, which if my healing was completed, became totally illogical to me.

"I am trying to tell you that perception and reality are one and the same. Pain is the illusion that is brought into reality by a belief system that allows pain. If you change the belief system, the response, the symptoms will change," he said.

"You say you have trusted you are healed and therefore should no longer be experiencing pain," he continued. "The messages are sent to the body through a complex process that is complicated to explain. Suffice it to say that the symptoms of years of one belief sometimes takes a little longer to wipe out and free from the body than a person who is healed may like.

"The connection with the pain often takes a while longer to be completely severed from all the cells of the body; and the memory of the belief must be eradicated from each and every cell involved in the pain before the pain can completely disappear.

"Remember when I explained to you that you experience pain because you have not fully let go of the pain and hurt in your heart? I told you that your past-life traumas have frightened you, kept you from fulfilling your true role as a woman. Childbearing, pregnancy is the ultimate definition of womanhood and you have suffered much due to your psychic ability and your femininity, your womanhood, in many lifetimes.

"You understand this now a bit more since you have seen, and actually relived, the fear and suffering you experienced in those lifetimes during some of your regressions."

I listened intently as he continued.

"The hurt will go away if you think joyful thoughts and are open to reminding yourself as often as possible that a healing has been completed. These two attitudes together work very well to speed up the process of eradicating the idea of pain from the cells involved, for it is the idea that created the pain in the first place.

"In addition, it is always good to envision healing light energy entering the body and surrounding the body like a cocoon, as you did early this morning in your healing exercise you learned from Louise," he said.

After channeling my healing guide, I sat quietly, meditating for quite a while. I thought about all the things he had just said, and had previously shared with me, about healing in general and my problems in particular. I tried to be positive, as he had suggested.

Even though I was in pain, which made it difficult to concentrate on other things, I tried to draw the healing light energy from the universe to form a halo around my entire body, and tried to be at peace. I noticed that whenever I did this, I felt considerably better.

I felt more positive also, as things seemed to be moving in the right direction. There was a lot more involved in healing than I had previously realized and I was starting to understand much more about the entire process.

~ 7 ~

A New Guide, A New Insight

A couple of weeks went by and I found that as the sun came and went with each passing day, I still had many questions about all that I had been experiencing and learning from channeling my guides, and also from my extraordinary visits to the Lodge of Women. The new world I had recently opened up to was creating some confusion and I needed some answers. I continued with my daily meditations. I asked also for help from a higher source.

It was at this time that I began receiving messages from a new voice, one I had not heard before. He came through one day, loud and clear, saying:

"Rosalee, I am the Christ, the one you call Jesus of Nazareth. I have been called by many names ~ The Prince of Peace, Light of the World, King of the Jews and Savior of Mankind."

Jesus explained that my confusion was for a reason, which I would come to understand. He also said that he would like my help in writing a book.

"I am here to rewrite the Book of Miracles in a format that will be more easily understood. The Book has been written many ways and times and in many languages, although for this discussion, the one published as *"A Course in Miracles"* has been written but once. I will impart similar knowledge and information as some of the other books, but in a manner, a format, more conducive to the world in which you now live, Rosalee."

This, book will be called "It Has Always Been Thus: A Revised Look at *A Course in Miracles*."

Jesus explained that I had been chosen for several reasons, one being the fact that my purpose in this life is to share spiritual knowledge with many. The message of this book would be very clear and concise, and as this is my writing style, as seen in my newspaper writing and editing, Jesus felt I would be a worthy author.

He also felt that I would be a good author because I had never compromised the integrity of a story in order to boost readership. And last, but certainly not the least of my qualifications, was what Jesus called, "Your natural ability to channel thoughts from those of us in the higher realms." He said, "This ability is second-nature to you now, Rosalee."

Jesus said that this book could not be completed, however, until another book I would write regarding my experiences in the Lodge of Women and all I had been learning from my guides had been published.

Jesus told me, as Louise also had, that there was much for me to relearn and experience in order to make me completely ready for my life's work. In order for me to share the knowledge, I had to relearn it and also learn many new concepts as well.

This all seemed a bit overwhelming. I went blank. Overwhelmed. That was the word. And beyond that, I was silent. I think I had suddenly become a writer who was at a loss for words to express all that I was feeling.

~ 8~

A Healing Dream

During the next ten days I continued to meditate and channel, getting a great deal of information from Jesus that would be part of the second book, the one which would be written with my help.

I had also been putting into practice all the things I was learning, or re-learning, as my guides like to say. One night in particular I practiced my healing meditation again, the same way I had been taught during my visit to the Lodge of Women. The next morning I awakened remembering a healing dream.

I am sitting outdoors in a field of low grass, and the breeze is gentle. There are mountains all around in the distance, for 360 degrees. A dog comes out of nowhere and walks up to me, barking. Then he sits beside me quietly.

"Wisdom is found from observation, watching, seeing from a place of quietness and calm," he says. "Watching as if from a distance even though you may be in the midst of confusion. In this you will find wisdom, for by detaching yourself from the situation, you will see as

clearly as eagles and you will know what is the right thing to do or say."

It would be about four days later before I would fully comprehend the wisdom and the clarity the dog was trying to impart so carefully in my dream. And then, as if a spark finally ignited and illuminated the whole picture, it suddenly became very clear. It was the reason Jesus had mentioned to me and also would not clarify. It was the fact that my confusion was necessary because that confusion was the very thing that created the impetus for me to ask for guidance from a higher level, a higher source.

Without the desire for communication on a higher level, I would never have heard Jesus when he came to me. This has made my path clearer, for although I don't fully understand where it is all leading, there is a sense, a knowing from the quality of the information I am receiving, that this is indeed my life's work. I have found my true path, my destiny.

When I realized this, Jesus came through again saying, "I am pleased you have found the reason why all your confusion was necessary. I have told you there is a reason for everything and now you have seen this for yourself."

It was at about this time that Mike and I started planning another trip to Arizona and thought maybe an adventure into California may be interesting as well. As it was after we had planned our first trip to Arizona last year, we began having conversations with people who suggested places we might visit in California. Especially mentioned for their pristine beauty were the redwood forests. We grew more and more interested each time we talked to another person until finally we decided to split our trip between Arizona and California.

A couple of days later I began channeling messages from Jesus relating to our trip and the idea of getting away from Miami for a while and spending time "relaxing in some high energy places out west." He also mentioned visiting Louise. "I am pleased you have planned to visit there again," were the words that Jesus had used.

Three nights later, I was still trying to adjust to all of this, when I thought about meeting Louise as I was falling asleep. I knew that I was in for another Dreamtime adventure into the mystical world of the Lodge of Women.

I am in the wooden Lodge and Louise's back is to me. She turns to face me and greets me.

"I am glad you are here my child. It has been a very long time and I am glad you are visiting and we are here together now. I am pleased you have come and there is so much we have to discuss and much to share and learn."

As I began to recall this visit the next day, Jesus came through with a request.

"I am Jesus of Nazareth and I wish to hear and know what happened in the Lodge of Women, if I may?"

This was interesting as it confirmed what the Chief had told me, that the Lodge of Women and all the activities taking place there, is just that ~ a place for women ~ and that male entities were not allowed to enter there. It was all right for them to know and help me understand what went on if I wished, but the actual "place of spirit," as the Chief called it, was somehow off limits to any one who is not a woman. In fact, the Lodge of Women is only open to women who are members of the secret society known as the Society of Women Healers. I agreed, and continued with my recollection of my Dreamtime visit.

"I know much has happened since our last meeting and I am here with you now to help make sense of everything ~ of all that has transpired," Louise says.

"Will you now lie down my dear," she continues, "And I will help to clear the chakras for you and open up the energy fields."

She gazes into my eyes.

"I will tell you all that you need to know. Did you know that I am wise beyond my years?" she says, and gives me a wry smile.

"I have many things to teach you this early morning and it will be a long visit for us together now."

Suddenly, I am lying on a tall wooden bed, more like a tall bench or table, and Grandma begins laying stones on and near my body at the areas of the chakra centers.

She starts by my head on the table and lays an amethyst, a smooth lavender colored amethyst. Next she picks up a darker colored, circular-shaped amethyst which looks flattened on opposite sides. She places one of the flat sides at the center of my forehead right between the eyes, in the area of the third eye chakra.

In the area of the throat chakra she lays a light blue, translucent aquamarine and a darker, opaque blue lapis lazuli to open communication.

"This will help you communicate better with all those around you and with whom you come in contact," she says. "I am pleased with your communication skills now, and these can only improve and continue to improve as you walk through this life, my dear daughter, my granddaughter and friend across time."

Then she concentrates her attention on the heart chakra and places an emerald there.

"It is good that you wear emeralds, Rosalee. The love they bring is good and they open up and give away to you, and you are open to receiving their gifts. It is a good marriage, a good combination for you, my dear.

"Now that we are at the yellow navel chakra, what will we use?" she asks, and then immediately answers her own question.

"I like the citrine and you like it too. It is a good, strong stone for you and one that will help to ease your tensions and quiet and calm your emotions in order that you may learn and grow more easily. It will help you to stay calm and centered even in the midst of danger or a storm of confusion. It is a strong centering and balancing stone for you and your emotions. Your healing guide has advised you well to get a tourmaline of green and yellow. The yellow would be the citrine, and married with the green tourmaline, it is a very powerful balancer for you.

"The tourmaline offers clarity of vision and the citrine quiets the emotions and therefore allows you to have clarity of thought as well. It is a powerful and healing combination of stones for you and it will be very good for you to get one of these."

She puts the stone on my navel, the area of the navel chakra, which controls the emotions.

"I think that a green and yellow tourmaline will be a wonderful addition to the stones you now carry and wear. Wear one, if you would like, and it will bring you much luck and strength and fortune in your healing abilities, both for yourself and for your healing for others. It will be a very good stone for you to wear and even carry, but wearing will make it more powerful for you."

I notice that the stone, which she has placed on the navel chakra, has more yellow than green, almost a half-and-half stripe of yellow and green, but with the yellow stripe being just a bit larger than the green. I think of how pleased I am with this knowledge, as Louise continues.

"Now the orange seeds and the fruit, as you know, are representative of the womb of woman, filled with the seeds of creativity and new life," she says.

I'm not sure exactly how she has done it, but there is an orange in her hands in one instant and then it is cut into halves in the next. She places one half, open side down on my belly, the area of the reproductive chakra, and continues to speak.

"Yours is the womb of all women, the womb of creativity. The creativity of all the universe belongs to you, my daughter.

"Now, let us continue with the opening and strengthening of your other chakras," she says, and lays a garnet at the base chakra, resting it on the pubic bone.

"To keep you grounded and align the spine, to keep you in perfect health, my dear, a garnet is a good thing for you to carry. At all times, you will feel grounded, close to the earth, if you will keep a garnet or a ruby close to you," she says, as she continues.

"I will again put a carnelian between the ankles, as it is a strong stone and a good one for you. If you see one that you feel especially attracted to, it will be good for you to wear or carry this one at all times. It is a good balancer and strong healer and has good medicine for you. It will help strengthen you for the work you are doing and will do and accomplish on this earth walk.

"I will be well pleased if I see you are wearing a carnelian when you visit me again in the Lodge."

Louise gazes into my eyes.

"Now you are balanced and will have the strength to accomplish your work, my dear daughter," she says.

"I know you are planning another visit to Arizona. Look for me there and visit me again soon in the Lodge, whenever you wish."

And with that, the scene disappears and I am back, awakening in my room.

A day later, after my usual routine of a short meditation, I began channeling. The now familiar voice again came through loud and clear.

"I am Christ, Rosalee, the one you call Jesus of Nazareth. I am with you now because I have some things to talk about with you."

He talked about many things including my ability to channel even while I am involved in other tasks and how this works.

"We use your quietness, the quietness of your energy, to communicate our thoughts and often our wisdom and knowledge to you as well.

"I am telling you this because you are about to embark on a journey where you will see and experience many wondrous things. There will be spectacles of the sort of stuff which men only dream of, and you will be an integral part of these wondrous experiences.

"Do not be afraid or nervous, my dear Rosalee," Jesus continued. "I know you view these gifts of channeling and communication as well as your insights, not as a gift at times but as a responsibility to all those around you, your fellow man and mankind in general."

I heard something more and wondered if I was hearing correctly when Jesus interrupted my thoughts.

"You are hearing me very well when I say you will be a catalyst, Rosalee, as many will consider the experiences you are bringing to light as a sign from above. It is a sign that they should change their ways and be more child-like in their acceptance of things they may not understand or fully comprehend.

"This will start with Mike and ripple out to all who you know and all who know you; and many more will want to get to know you.

"If you go to visit Louise, go to her and greet her as your grandma, your mother and friend across time. She will respond to you in kind. Then you will know that there is a reason you have met and have again come together in this place, and that it is the right place for you and for your learning and growth.

"She may want to share a ritual with you, now long-ago forgotten by you, Rosalee, but which you knew well and performed a long time ago in your past lives as an American Indian. This will help you to heal others, much the same way as you have done in your past lives as a healing woman. You have been a renowned and powerful healer with insights and abilities to see far into the future and into the past," Jesus said.

"These abilities again are starting to return, and will continue to do so, as you learn the necessary steps to take in order to bring about the memory of these past lives and abilities. You will restore the healing knowledge and seeing capabilities, which you many times have been well renowned for, Rosalee.

"I know you do not feel confident in your abilities now as a seer or as a healer," Jesus continued, "But you will gain a tremendous amount of confidence in yourself, and respect from others, just during the time you are in Arizona.

"And this confidence and respect shall and will continue to grow. You will see signs of it as you go through California. And when you visit the redwood forest, you will have a vision and see what your life is truly all about."

I began to feel somewhat intimidated by all I was hearing ~ not just some of these things which I'd previously been told by my guides, but now, that I would be seeing a special vision as well ~ but Jesus brought me back to his thoughts as he continued.

"I am telling you these things not to frighten you but to prepare you for the great and tremendous growth which lies just ahead of you as you walk this path of life with us by your side, Rosalee.

"It is a good trip for you to take and will be a learning experience for you, and you will be able to teach others much of what you have learned, are learning and will learn on this trip.

"You already know much but there is much more to learn and you will learn and grow, and in this process of learning and growing you will teach others much of what they need to know and do with their lives."

I listened and took careful notes as Jesus continued.

"I am again telling you these things, Rosalee, not to frighten you but to prepare you and give you a little advance notice so you can know what is just ahead for you in the very near future. This will be such an exciting time for you. You are embarking on a trip that will truly be a journey for you into the deeper realms of the world of spirit.

"You can rest assured that you will be safe, as none of this is dangerous in any way for you or anyone around you. It is and will always be filled with all goodness and light for you and for all others who are around you. They will automatically be filled with the joy and peace of the light that surrounds you, and it will be very pleasing and pleasant for them.

"There will be many who will want to spend time with you just bathing in or soaking up your aura, so to speak. This will not, cannot hurt you in any way, for you truly are a being of light, and goodness and light will always follow you everywhere and anywhere that you go.

"I have your best interests at heart, Rosalee, when I tell you these things, because you are very unaware of how others see you, and it is now time to realize that the light you have is attracting and will continue to attract a lot of people around you.

"I am certain you like this, for I know how much you like to help people," Jesus continued. "It is the purpose of your being born, coming into this life you are now living, Rosalee. And I and we, those who speak through me in the higher realms, can think of no one who helps others, and enjoys the mere thought of helping others, more than you."

I felt uneasy and more than a bit uncertain about all that I was hearing, but Jesus continued.

"I am delighted you are not convinced that much of what I am saying is true. This only means that you are seeing the world right now through your eyes, which have a different vision and perception than our eyes. We see the big picture and how everything and everyone relates to everything and everyone else. It is how it is in the higher realms of consciousness.

"I am glad you hear me so well and understand what I say so completely, Rosalee. I am with you always, until the end of time, if there is such a thing as time, and I love you and all the children of the world, and you are child-like in your innocence and this is what I love most about you. You are here with us so that we may guide and teach you and help you to grow in order that you may fulfill your life's purpose of sharing this knowledge with many. It is how it is."

~ 9 ~

Exploring Life's Purpose

I went through the rest of the day in a state of confusion. I did my work for our business in order to get ready for the trip, which was now less than two weeks away. All the while I couldn't help but think of what Jesus had said, and about how so many of these things about my abilities and my life's work were practically the same exact words I had been hearing from Louise in the Lodge. Indeed, very much the same information as I'd received from all of my other guides as well, for almost as long as I had been channeling.

It's as if they were all trying to give me the same message, and I couldn't seem to make sense of it in my life. It all seemed so foreign in a way, and in many other ways, it all seemed so familiar. At times it seemed as though I didn't know who I was or how I felt about all my recent experiences. To say I was confused was a tremendous understatement.

I went to bed that evening with this sense of confusion, and then I felt something else altogether. It was that now familiar pull of the soul rising from the body, taking flight for another Dreamtime excursion. I relaxed and allowed myself to fall asleep, knowing I would be visiting Louise.

I am in the Lodge and Louise turns to face me.

"Will you let me help you, Rosalee, put the pieces of your life together? I will show you where and how everything fits together if you wish."

"Yes, Grandma," I say. "I want to know what is happening and understand what it all means."

"Well, let us begin," Louise says, and looks into my eyes with a little bit of a smile.

"You see, it is a matter of what you want and that which you have asked for in this lifetime and beyond, into the past, the time before you came into this life, that will determine and has determined what your experiences in this life shall be," she says.

"Rosalee, you have chosen as your main purpose in this life a good and noble purpose, and that is to share knowledge with many. This you will do from what you already know and have already learned, and from what you will know in the near future, my child.

"I am proud to be the one to help you, or actually, one of the ones who are helping and will continue to help you. We are helping you in your endeavor to learn and grow so that you may and will, in turn, give back and share this knowledge with many.

"I am proud to be sharing the journey of this lifetime, to share this earth walk with you my daughter, my granddaughter and friend across time. I am proud and pleased to be part of your growing knowledge, and I will always remember fondly these visits that we have shared and will continue to share together in the Lodge of Women. I am very pleased, my child.

"Now I will explain to you about the things that have happened recently in your life, and I am honored to be able to be the one who gets to explain these things to you.

"I will tell you what you are facing when you are ready to come to grips with the future that is yours. Yours to live and become. Yours to grow into and be all you can be, my child."

I look at her, not sure at all that I want to hear any more than I have already, but she interrupts my thoughts.

"I will tell you, if you are ready now, or I will wait if you prefer, until another time when you feel that you are ready to learn your true potential and face your destiny head on and look it squarely in the eye."

"I'm not sure, Grandma," I say, hesitantly. "I think I want to see what there is in my future, but I'm afraid. Maybe that means I should wait."

"It is your choice my dear Birdy Rose, but I will tell you this much. It is not a future you can run from or hide from, but it is also not a future to be feared.

"A good life will be yours and a very good future is ahead of you my dear. I shall continue if you would like to know more. It shall be my pleasure to inform you of what the future holds, what there is already in the making and what lies ahead for you, if you wish. Shall I continue?"

"Oh, yes, Grandmother," I say, now eager to hear and know what would be my future, my destiny. "I am eager to hear, please tell me more."

"Well, it is a bright future indeed," Louise continues, "a bright future, indeed.

"There will be much revelry and merry-making about the good news which your books will impart. The wisdom and knowledge that was lost to your people will be regained and you will be heralded, lauded as a good person who will lead with the truth and conquer the fear of

lives drained of spirituality and souls searching for the way back home. And you will lead them and show them the way through your books. It is a gift that you are a writer, and a very good one at that, and it will be your way of sharing your new-found knowledge with many.

"It is your life's purpose for this life," she continues. "You have chosen to share knowledge with many. And it is a gift you will deliver well. You are a good writer and people will enjoy reading what you have to say. The way you say what you have to say will be interesting and enlightening and will fill many hearts with the joy and peace of the oneness of God.

"And it is good for you and will also be good for all those who are touched by your work," she says, obviously seeing a hint of recognition in my eyes, for she continues, answering my unspoken question.

"And you are familiar with this idea and these words, for they are the very words you wrote to describe how you felt about your spiritual work and your poetry not yet three years ago. And it will come to be and is coming into fruition even as we speak, my daughter.

"Everything is unfolding as it should, a concept from the "Desiderata," which you also love, and I am pleased to see that you understand so well the nature of the universe and all there is around us. But it is not surprising, however, for you have been in this spiritual realm for so many lifetimes that there are aspects of spirituality and spiritual communication that are truly second nature to you now, Rosalee.

"I am talking of your communication with your higher guide, the Christ Jesus of Nazareth, and with your other helper and healing guides and other people's guides as well. This ability will continue to grow and flourish and will make you welcome anywhere you go on this earth.

"And you will visit many places, my dear, and see and be a part of many wondrous things. Your life will work well for you, you will see.

"Things will just work out well for you, and it will be as you would have it. It will be as you would wish for if you were to sit down and think of how you would like things in your life to turn out, and even how you would like your life in general to work. It will all be as you would have wished."

My memory of this Dreamtime visit ended abruptly, without the usual good-byes, and I couldn't help thinking that there was more to this visit, something Louise might have told me that I didn't want to hear. Anyway, I couldn't remember a thing more about this journey into the spiritual realm.

The ten days until our vacation passed quickly, with just enough time for business preparations and packing, and little or no time for meditating or even any quiet time for being alone with my own thoughts.

I had not mentioned to Mike any of the exceptionally extraordinary things I had been hearing about our trip from my channeling with Jesus or my Dreamtime visits in the Lodge with Louise. Somehow, I think I didn't want to believe any of it was real myself, and not talking about it somehow gave it less credence.

Our plans included a week's stay in Arizona and then a week in California, and we were now on a plane, bound for Phoenix.

Once we arrived at Phoenix, we completed our car rental arrangements and headed north toward Sedona. While there we would be staying with Ron and Deanna, friends whom we had met last year. They are both spiritual healers, and the very first time we met it became apparent that there was a sort of special bond between us. Though they are my parents' age and have children about my age, we have a tremendous amount in common, spiritual aspects being just one of them.

The ride north from the Phoenix airport filled us with the spirit of the Southwest. Cactus was everywhere to be found, on all the roadsides and hillsides leading out of the city. The backdrop of the bluish-gray mountains was spectacular. As we left the city, the sagebrush and colorful desert wildflowers grew among the many varieties of prickly cactus, the taller ones standing like people with their arms outstretched greeting us from the mountainsides.

We played our newly purchased cassette of Billy Joel's "*River of Dreams,*" and drove through the wide-open spaces, our eyes delighted by the natural beauty all around us. This was going to be an exciting trip and we had just begun to feel relaxed and at ease. Later we listened to some of our cassettes of Native American flute music and enjoyed the ride.

About an hour-and-a-half into our two-and-a-half - hour ride, the terrain changed dramatically. No longer was there cactus. The land was now green and more forest-like as we left the desert, and we could see the familiar red-rock mountain ranges ahead of us in the distance. The change in scenery and especially the mountain ranges were a feast for our eyes.

Finally we arrived in Sedona and drove through the town and out again, going north into the Village of Oak Creek. We drove for a while longer before pulling over at a service station to give Deanna a call. She had been waiting for us and, as I thought, we were just a few blocks away form the house that she and her husband had recently moved into. She gave me directions, and Mike and I were quickly on our way to renew our friendship and explore the area once again.

Deanna greeted us at the door with a big smile and great big hugs. She showed us around her home, which had exquisite views of the red-rock mountains from the living room, bedrooms and kitchen. Deanna showed us where we'd be staying and we unpacked the car and got situated in our room. Ron was expected home any minute, and we had all planned to go out to dinner.

Ron walked in just as we were finishing our organizing. I'd forgotten how tall he is, and raised up on my tiptoes to give him a big hug. We all dressed for the evening and headed out to a restaurant, where we talked late into the night. Mike and I became very tired and realized we had flown through a three-hour time difference. It may have been midnight in Arizona, but it still felt like 3 a. m. to us.

We got back to Deanna and Ron's and snuggled up for a long night's sleep.

To my surprise, I awakened with the morning light. It must have been about 6:30 a.m., Arizona time. I walked into the living room and enjoyed the view of the interplay of light and shadows on the red mountains just outside the windows. There was something about this land that lifted my spirits and made me feel like I could soar. The energy here was very good, and I looked forward to a wonderful trip.

Deanna awakened shortly afterward. We shared the quiet of the morning light as I sipped my herbal tea and she enjoyed her morning coffee. It wasn't long before Mike and Ron were also up and we shared a few moments before Deanna and Ron both left for work. We told them of our plan to spend the day exploring the high-energy vortex areas for which Sedona is popular and then get together with them in the evening for dinner.

That morning we explored one of the vortex areas, a quiet, peaceful place known for its balance of male and female energies. We spent time sitting quietly, meditating, just enjoying the beauty and taking in the energy. The beautiful red-rock mountains all around us made an exquisite backdrop to the picturesque scenery. We enjoyed relaxing on a blanket under the shade of the beautiful, tall pine trees, listening to the sound of the leaves rustling overhead as they swayed in the breeze.

Afterward, we were more than ready for lunch and headed out to a local restaurant, stopping along the way to say hello to the tour guide who had shown us the vortex sites on our trip last year. We seemed to feel an unusual bond with her as well, which I would normally think was rather strange, but which more recently I'd begun to just accept, trusting my intuition and going with my feelings.

She was happy to see us and joined us for hamburgers. We talked about some of the unusual coincidences that occurred on our trip last year, and filled her in on a little bit of my recent Dreamtime explorations.

We agreed to keep in touch and she pointed us in the right direction, drawing a makeshift map on a paper napkin to show us the way to Airport Mesa, another of the high-energy vortex sites. The vortex sites are said to be at the intersection of the earth's ley lines, thus the reason for the high energy. When there, one can really feel a difference in the energies. It's a special feeling that makes me want to return again and again. The entire town seems to be permeated with the same kind of energy, only less concentrated.

After we soaked up the energy of Airport Mesa, we stopped off in town once again to pick up a gift to take for Louise. The next day we were going to visit Louise and her family at the Canyon de Chelly. Deanna and Ron had never been to Spider Rock so the four of us were going to make an adventure of the nearly seven-hour drive to Chinle.

We bought a gift of hand-made wind chimes and headed back to our base at Deanna and Ron's to relax for a while before packing some things. Ron and Deanna were there and we became quickly involved in conversation. I told them a little about my Dreamtime meetings with Louise in the Lodge of Women, recounting some of the details. The anticipation was building, as none of us knew quite what to expect, and I, most of all, was still more than a little confused about my visits to the Lodge.

We enjoyed a late dinner and got ready for bed, packing in between.

Morning came quickly and we had just enough time to get dressed and finish packing, bringing along provisions for the road, which in Arizona always means plenty of drinking water. I was thirstier than ever in the arid climate of the Southwest.

Everything prepared, including the water and some snacks for the road, and we were ready to head north out of town. We all packed into the rental car with Mike at the wheel and Ron, map in hand, navigating from behind, and drove off. None of us knew what to expect, but there was a sense, a feeling in the air that we were headed for a very unusual adventure.

~ 10 ~

Visiting Spider Rock

We drove for a couple of hours across varied terrain, some rich with forest vegetation, and other areas very arid and rocky with little sign of any growth, even the cactus. I began to get contemplative, thinking about some of the things I had recently learned in the Dreamtime and from my channeling with Jesus. I also knew that I had made two Dreamtime visits to the Lodge of Women within the past few days and had not taken the time to sit quietly and recall my experiences.

Suddenly something triggered a memory and I was again reliving the first of those Dreamtime visits. I let myself drift off as Mike, Deanna and Ron continued their conversation.

Louise is greeting me, turning around to face me in the Lodge. She is looking at me with that now familiar, kind, loving look in her eyes.

"I am glad you are here, my dear. I have many things to talk to you about. I will begin by saying that this trip you are going on will be an exciting one for you. There will be many wondrous things to see and experience. When

you visit Spider Rock, everyone will be happy to see you and there will be a celebration in your honor.

"Also, I will tell you, do not be bothered by having not brought any earrings on this trip. You do not have to buy any either. You will be given a gift when you visit Louise and her family in Chinle. They will have a gift of earrings for you."

My awareness slipped back to the car in which I was riding and to the present. What she had said about the earrings caught my interest. When I first arrived in Arizona I realized that I had not brought earrings with me on the trip. I had even thought about trying to find a pair that I liked when I visited the local shops. Yesterday, however, I began to feel that it was not necessary to look for earrings ~ that I would somehow get a pair without looking for them. I couldn't help feeling just a bit amazed at how my visits to the Dreamtime permeated my everyday thoughts.

I let myself drift off again, but that fragment was all I could remember of that particular visit to the Lodge of Women.

I began to recall another visit, one that occurred just last night. Again I only seemed to remember fragmentary glimpses of my experiences there.

"There will be much interest in all you have experienced in the Dreamtime, in the Lodge of Women, and they will be excited," Grandma is saying. "A ritual will be performed in your honor and there will be a feast, a celebration afterward."

Again I was aware of being in the car and in the present. That was all I was able to recall. A sense of confusion came over me, and I just couldn't, or maybe didn't want to, make sense of it all. Even more disturbing was the fact that I knew I hadn't remembered the entire visits, only small bits and pieces.

I began to wonder if my imagination was somehow running wild. Strangely enough, although I had been a newspaper reporter and column writer, I had always thought that I would never be able to write a novel because my imagination was not very good.

I knew I was considered excellent at reporting, but always felt I lacked the ability to make up stories out of my own imagination. Now I found myself questioning if all these very mystical and sometimes bizarre things I had been experiencing were brought about by my own imagination. I was just feeling insecure and very confused. I said nothing to Mike, Deanna or Ron, but joined in the conversation once again. The feeling of confusion was something I couldn't shake.

"Maybe," I thought to myself, "When I see Louise in person, she'll help me to understand, make sense of all that has been going on in my life and in my Dreamtime visits."

It was mid-afternoon when we approached the town of Chinle and drove along the town's main street leading to the Canyon de Chelly. I was anxious to see the magnificent obelisk of Spider Rock amidst the backdrop of the extremely peaceful red rock canyon. We parked the car at the overlook point, got out and walked along the trail. There it was in all its splendor ~ an awe-inspiring vision out in front of us, emerging from the Canyon floor.

"I see why you liked it here," Deanna said, looking at me. "You can feel the peacefulness here. It's a really special feeling ~ a good energy."

I looked at her and nodded. We stood silently for a few minutes, just taking in the view and the energy.

I began to pray for an understanding of all that I had been experiencing, when I suddenly realized I had wandered off the trail and onto the wooded mountain ridge just beyond. It was then that I began hearing the now familiar voice. It was Louise, my Grandma of the Dreamtime, but somehow I was channeling her thoughts. I listened as she spoke.

"I am glad to see you here again my granddaughter, my daughter and friend across time ~ glad you have come back to this very special place you remember flying over in your dream not that long ago. I have taught you much since that time and you will learn much on this trip, my child. Do not be afraid. It is your destiny. I have longed to see you here again. I am happy, my dear, very happy indeed."

Her words came through to me with such a wonderfully tranquil feeling that it put me at ease. However, as soon as her message had been heard, an uneasy confusion again began to fill my being. I had many questions.

Was that really Louise? I thought to myself. Or was I beginning to imagine things? If it was Louise, then am I somehow communicating telepathically with her, or how else could I hear her voice as though I were channeling her thoughts? I felt more confused than ever, and was even more hesitant to tell anyone what I was experiencing. I worked my way back through the woods and to the clearing of the path where Mike, Deanna and Ron were waiting.

"Let's go visit Louise and her family," I said to Mike, my anxiety showing. We walked back to the car and headed for the fifteen-minute ride to Louise's house. I could hardly wait to see them all, hardly wait to get some answers. I felt so confused I could hardly think.

We arrived at Louise's home and were greeted with a smile by the granddaughter, Dawn, whom we had met with Louise in the coin laundry last year. She would be 15 now. She had seen our car pull up and had walked across from her house which was just next door, wearing blue jeans and a T-shirt, her long dark hair flowing.

The entire family lived in a cluster of houses all grouped near to Louise's. It appeared to be a traditional living arrangement, although the homes ranged from the very traditional log *hogan*, reserved now mostly for ceremonial use, to the very modern double-wide trailer home, with variations of simple homes in between. We introduced Deanna and Ron and explained that we had come to visit Louise and the family.

"Wait," she said. "My Grandma will be back soon."

We hadn't arrived two minutes, hadn't even gone inside, when an old pick-up truck rolled into the dirt driveway. The passenger door opened and out came a petite lady, dressed in her colorful traditional clothing, her long hair pulled back neatly in a bun. Mike walked toward her and greeted her.

"Louise," he said.

She looked at him, a hint of recognition in her eyes. She turned to look at me. " Oh!" she said with a big smile, throwing her hands up in surprise. She walked toward me and hugged me tightly, burying her head in my shoulder. My eyes welled up with tears and my heart gladdened with excitement. There truly was a special bond here. We hugged for a moment longer and then she greeted Mike with a hello.

"We wanted to come and see you again," I said, as her granddaughter translated. "I have a lot to talk to you about. Have I been meeting with you in the Dreamtime?"

Louise uttered her response in her native Navajo to her granddaughter. "My Grandma says to come inside and we can talk," she said.

I walked along beside Louise who kept looking at me and smiling, her delight showing in her face.

We entered her simple yet cozy house to find a living room full of people. There was Louise's husband, Fred, a strapping man who looked like he was in his 60s. He had been driving the pick-up truck and had entered the house without uttering a word to us. He was sitting in a large brown chair, which was opposite a small sofa on which their daughter Dottie was seated. We had met Dottie last year when she and Louise had shown us Spider Rock and the other holy sites of the Canyon. There was Dottie's sister, Linda, and there was a young man who appeared to be in his 30s and who was introduced to us as Patrick, Linda's boyfriend. Dawn pulled up a chair behind the sofa where the others sat.

Mike introduced Deanna and Ron and we all sat on the long couch, which formed an L-shape in the living room adjacent to the shorter sofa. Mike sat to my left on the end, closest to the other couch on which Patrick was sitting. I sat next to Mike with Louise sitting beside me, Deanna on her right, and Ron next to her. I took out the wind chimes I'd bought for Louise and gave them to her. She opened the box and the entire family seemed pleased with the gift and the tones that it made.

We were told that Patrick speaks perfect English and would help us translate. Mike looked at me, but saw that I didn't know where to begin.

"We're here, he said, because Rosalee has been having some dreams she can't quite understand. She thinks she has been meeting with Louise and that Louise has been teaching her many of the Indian traditions."

Patrick translated in Navajo, and Fred seemed to reply. Patrick looked at me.

"What kind of Indian traditions?" he asked.

"Things related to healing and harmony with nature," I said. "She sometimes performs rituals on me or teaches me how to see things the way the Indians have always done. She says I have done these things before and she is only re-teaching me what I already know."

Patrick again translated and this time both Louise and Fred seemed to have some understanding, or recognition, as they both spoke to Patrick in response. Louise was nodding. Again Patrick turned his attention to me.

"Who is it that is teaching you these things?" he asked.

"I thought it was Louise, but I'm not sure," I tried to explain through all my confusion. "I know that it's an Indian woman. She told me she was Louise, and she looks like Louise in a way, but then somehow not like Louise at all, but I thought it was Louise in spirit."

Patrick again translated and again everyone waited in silence for a response from Fred and Louise. They spoke in Navajo, with Louise speaking and nodding, signifying at least some sort of understanding to what I was trying to explain. She was holding my hand against her knee, and I knew she felt comfortable having me with her.

Patrick looked at me again. "What kinds of rituals. Can you explain them?" he said.

"Well," I began, "Different things each time I have a visit to the Lodge of Women." I explained what I had been told about the Lodge and also explained about how Louise, or the woman I thought of as Louise, balanced my chakras using many different colored stones and crystals, placing them at the chakra points on my body.

I told about the time she crushed the crystal and tourmaline and smudged the mixture on my eyelids and at the point of the third-eye chakra and across my forehead and said it was to help me have clarity of vision and clarity of thought.

Patrick translated and came back with more questions, still no answers as yet for me. "What else did she show you?" he asked.

"She showed me a crystal and told me I could look into a crystal or into someone's eyes and know their future, and she said I have done this very well before in other lives."

Again Patrick translated, and without any reaction, looked at me again.

"And what else did she show you?"

"We walked in the woods during my Dreamtime visit and she taught me how to learn from nature, from all that is around us. She taught me that nature will teach everything, if we know how to be in harmony with all that is around us, to be quiet and see the lessons that nature has to offer," I said.

Once again Patrick translated, and again, the only responses forthcoming were from Louise and Fred, in Navajo. I felt like I had opened up a puzzle, spilling all the pieces on the living room floor and they were trying their best to help me find all the pieces to make the picture fit together clearly. I was still a little nervous and very confused.

"These rituals you describe are the same ones our medicine men perform," Patrick said with conviction. "We think that what these dreams are telling you is that you should find an Indian woman, a Native American person you are drawn to, like Louise, in order to help you understand. We think you need to have a Blessing Way done for you. It is a special ceremony and it will help clear up the meaning of your dreams for you."

I looked at Mike and he looked at me. I didn't know what to think.

"What does that involve?" Mike asked.

"You need to find a medicine man and talk to him. Rosalee can tell him all of the things that have happened in her dreams, and he will see if he wants to perform the Blessing Way," Patrick said.

I felt nervous although I didn't know why. The information I had told them about was received without any hint of it being strange or odd to them. So well received, in fact, that I should probably have been extremely calm. Maybe it was the silence, the quiet, that made me wonder just what exactly was being *thought* about all the things I had told them, which was making me feel insecure. Somehow I wasn't so sure about the sound of all this. What exactly was a Blessing Way and how could it help?

I turned to Patrick with my fears. "What is the Blessing Way?" I said. "What will it do? How is it done?"

"It is a ritual that has been passed down in our Navajo tradition," he said. It is done with special prayers and it is done to help you understand, to clear up your confusion, to help you make sense of your dreams so you can be in harmony."

Then it hit me. I remembered what I had recently heard in the Dreamtime from someone who, if she wasn't Louise, I was now wondering who she was.

"I just remembered, I was told that when I came here to visit, there would be a special ritual performed for me," I said, feeling very puzzled.

"Aah, you see!" he said, and then translated quickly what I had said. The room seemed instantly to resound with a collective sigh and nods of agreement. Everyone instantly had a smile on their faces ~ faces which just a moment before had all seemed so quiet and still with an earnest resolve toward listening to what I had been saying and helping me to fit the pieces of this puzzle together. They found the answer they were seeking.

"This is what I have been saying. You need to have a Blessing Way. It is what we think you need," Patrick said.

It took a couple of minutes for the excitement to quiet down, then Mike spoke.

"Well, what would we need to do? How would we go about having a Blessing Way done?" he asked.

Patrick looked resolved, with very little expression showing in his face. He had been this way the entire time he translated, not offering any expression of understanding or recognition about anything that I had said. I couldn't quite figure him out.

"You have to find a medicine man and talk to him. If he thinks it is right, he will suggest a Blessing Way. Then Rosalee would need to give him something of hers, not necessarily something of value, but something he will use when he prays and meditates on how he is to help her. He will receive a vision and know what is called for. He will tell you what his fees are and if there is anything else you will need," Patrick said.

"All right," said Mike. "Where do we find a medicine man. I think Rosalee would like to do this."

They looked at me. The whole family became very silent.

"Well," I said. "I'd at least like to talk to a medicine man and ask what he thinks, what his opinion might be."

Patrick looked me in the eyes.

"I am a medicine man," he said. "I can perform the Blessing Way for you."

I looked at him, shocked. He was like an expert poker player, one who would never tip his hand and whose face one could never read. I thought to myself, this mild-mannered translator is really a medicine man, and a young one at that. I looked at his dark brown eyes and his short hair. He was certainly not what I had pictured in a medicine man.

"So far, this trip is full of surprises," I said, shaking my head in amazement.

"Would you do a Blessing Way for me?" I asked.

"Yes," Patrick said.

"When can you do this?" I asked.

"I have a ceremony to perform tonight for a girl becoming a woman, but tomorrow morning after it is over, I will be able to do it for you."

He spoke in Navajo again, then addressed me. "You would normally need moccasins, but it will be all right. Just come here at about nine o'clock and we can start."

"Do we need to bring anything at all," I asked?

There was more talk in Navajo and this time it was Dawn who spoke.

"You can get some food for a lunch, a feast afterward. It will be like a holiday for us when we celebrate the Blessing Way," she said. "Make sure it is something you like and will eat, for if you don't eat, it will mean you will become sort of stingy. Everyone will eat afterward and celebrate."

Mike asked Dawn what the family might enjoy and they quickly decided on fried chicken, which we could pick up at the local grocery store along with the rest of the meal.

I remembered we had to arrange a fee, and that I was also expected to give Patrick something I owned so he could use it when he prayed.

I mentioned this to Mike and he quickly called Patrick aside. He agreed on a nominal fee. I thought of what I could give Patrick. I looked at a chain around my neck and opened the silver locket embellished with a carnelian, which I had just purchased a couple of days before in Sedona. Inside, I had placed three small garnets I had also purchased at the same time. I handed them to Patrick and told him they were garnets (something I'm sure he already knew, but I wasn't thinking clearly) and asked if they would be all right. He looked at them, holding them up to let the light pass through them.

"Yes," he said, nodding.

Just then Dottie walked up to me. "We want you to have this, Rosalee," she said. "They are dream catchers."

I looked at the silver earrings she had placed in my hands, and the memory hit me again. I looked at her, feeling a little like this was all a bit too amazing to be really happening.

"I was told in my Dreamtime visit that I would be given a present ~ a gift of earrings ~ when I visited Louise."

She looked at me, not saying a word, and then turned quickly to explain it all to a cousin who had just walked in and wanted to know what was going on.

"She has been having many dreams and Patrick is going to do the Blessing Way for her tomorrow," she explained.

I thanked her and hugged her before putting on the earrings.

Mike walked toward me. We were tired and it was time to leave. We would be returning in the morning. I still felt confused, but somehow I felt things would be better.

We said our good-byes and the four of us headed back into the car and drove toward the hotel in town where I had made reservations. We were hungry and had dinner in the hotel's restaurant before even registering for the night.

Afterward, we went directly to our rooms, which were across the hall from one another, and got ready for bed. I was exhausted and I had a feeling tomorrow would be a very big day.

~ 11 ~

The Blessing Way

The next morning I awakened remembering a Dreamtime visit to the Lodge of Women that answered some of my questions.

"Rosalee, I am glad you have come this night to visit here in the Lodge of Women. There is much to share with you, much for you to know and understand," Grandma is saying.

"I am confused," I say to her.

"I know, my child, that you are confused, and I will clear up the confusion for you. When I first met you in the Lodge, my dear Rosalee, you were with Louise, the woman you met on your first visit to Spider Rock and with whom you visited yesterday afternoon. You have known her before and she has been your grandmother, your mother and friend across time as I have led you to believe.

"I am the woman who glowed in that first dream you had with Louise my dear. I am White Buffalo Calf

Woman and I have known you many times and in many lifetimes as well. I tried to let you know who I was when we first met here in the Lodge, however you were not ready to believe or understand that you had a visit with an Indian holy person. The shaman who told you of me was correct. I had asked her to pass on the message of who I am, but you were not ready to hear.

"Nevertheless it was time to begin your learning ~ the re-learning of what you have known in other times ~ of your Indian heritage as a seer and healer and woman of much spiritual knowledge, knowledge of the universe. And I am glad you have been with me and I have been the one to help you regain this knowledge and be able to go forward with your life's work.

"It is your knowledge and your destiny that have brought you here together with me again in this lifetime. I and we, those of us in the higher realms, your other guides, felt it was all right to let you believe you were learning from Louise as she has taught you much in other lives. As I have said, she was your grandmother and teacher, and she has been a mother for you as well and a good friend across time, Rosalee.

"You have not been seeing me, looking at me closely. Look at me now, at my entire being," she says.

I take a step backward to really look at her.

"You're glowing," I say, in amazement. "You are the woman who glowed in my dream!"

She smiles at me and appears to glow even brighter than before.

"I am White Buffalo Calf Woman and I am your teacher in the Dreamtime. Whenever you have visited the Lodge of Women, it has been I who have been there with you teaching you, performing the ancient rituals for you that you may become aware and strong and regain all your

knowledge my dear. It is your time and your destiny now to share this knowledge with many, Rosalee.

"Today when you meet with the Medicine Man Patrick, tell him what I have told you. Also, tell him that I said he would have a new name for you. Your Indian name my dear is to be, Golden Eagle With a Torch on Its Wings, and he would have received this name for you during his meditations. It is a good name for you and one that has great meaning.

"Like the eagle spirit within you, you can and are able to soar above the madness of this world and see the larger, bigger picture as from an eagle's perspective. The torch you are carrying represents the enlightenment you are bringing to the people of the earth. It is a good name for you, a very good name indeed. You will wear a feather in your hair, and you will know what I tell you is truth.

"Tell the Medicine Man Patrick all these things I have told you when you see him, and tell him also that I have said I will not speak with you again until the time of the Blessing Way. Tell him also that I am aware that spirit talks through you. You are a channel for communication between the souls of the spirit realm, the great sky nation, and the Mother Earth, and I will be talking with you again during the ceremony.

"Tell him all these things as I have told you. Do not be afraid of telling him what I am saying and all I have said to you this night.

"Now, go my dear, for it is late and we both have a big day ahead of us. It will be an important day for you and for me. I am glad you have come to visit with me and I have been able to share my secret of who I am. Tell Patrick that I said there will be a blessing not only for you with the Blessing Way, but also blessings for all those who are present during the Blessing Way.

"It is a very good sign my dear. It is a sign of your growth. I am White Buffalo Calf Woman and I am well pleased. Now, go, before it gets too late."

The scene disappeared and I was awakening in the hotel room. I looked at Mike's watch. It was 7:05. I lay quietly for a while recalling my Dreamtime visit to the Lodge. I seemed to recall everything, but I was overcome with a feeling that Patrick the medicine man, and indeed everyone else, would think I was absolutely crazy when they heard all the things I was told in last night's visit.

Suddenly, a knocking at the door interrupted my thoughts.

"It's Ron. It's later than we thought. I forgot that on the reservation they observe Daylight Savings Time. It's almost 8:30."

"Okay," Mike called out, stirring from a deep sleep. "Thanks. We'll be ready soon."

When Patrick came into the living room, I called him aside to tell him all I could remember about my Dreamtime visit, as White Buffalo Calf Woman had instructed. It all seemed to be a blur now, although I remembered the important points.

I told him who she said she was, and what she had said about my name, the name he would have gotten for me in his meditations. I told him of the feather, and realized I was wearing a decorative comb in my hair, which was adorned with one large and two much smaller silver feathers. I told him what she had said about being aware that spirit talks through me and that she would not talk with me again until during the ceremony, and I told him of the blessings that she had said everyone who is present would receive.

This Patrick listened to with the same poker face he had shown yesterday. It made me so uneasy, because I had no idea what he was thinking, though I was convinced he was thinking that I must be crazy. He just listened and said, "O.K., O.K., O.K.," while nodding, to everything I said.

I felt like grabbing his shoulders and saying, "Don't say O.K.; tell me what you're thinking. Does all this sound plausible to you, or do you think I'm crazy?" I refrained, however, thinking that showing my insecurity would only make things worse.

Somehow I felt this was to be a peaceful day even though I was feeling so nervous, confused and out of sorts with my own being. I didn't know or understand any of this, but I felt like if this would help in any way, I was all for it.

Patrick signaled that it was time for us all to go over to the hogan, the traditional log home, now used mostly for ceremonial purposes. The hogan was octagonal and about twenty-five feet in diameter. The floor was barren earth, and in the center stood a large oil drum used to house the fire, which had just been started. Connected to it was a chimney pipe, which rose out of the top and up through the hogan's smoke hole.

Blankets were carefully laid out on the floor. We all sat around the fire, guests to one side, Louise's family to the other, and Louise, myself and Patrick toward the center. I was directly in front of the fire on the opposite side from the door. Great care was taken to see that I was seated on a blue blanket, and a purple blanket was draped around my shoulders. The colors were obviously very important. The door to the hogan was left open and a multicolored blanket was draped in the open doorway. Dottie explained that this was the traditional ceremonial blanket and that it is set out so anyone who would happen by would know not to interrupt the ceremony taking place inside.

With everything set, we were almost ready to begin. Patrick tied a headband around his head. Next, he opened a large medicine pouch and began taking out various objects and placing them carefully and neatly in rows on a blanket he had laid out to my right. He had a pipe, several crystals, a feather, and several smaller pouches, which I presumed contained herbs or other implements.

Then he sat quietly with his hands together in front of him for a couple of minutes. It looked like he was praying. He looked up at Louise and began speaking in the Navajo tongue. Then, in English, to Deanna and Ron, Mike and me, he indicated that we were ready to begin.

I was instructed to sit with my legs straight out in front of me.

Patrick unrolled a leather pouch, which he told us contained tobacco that he had gathered himself from a place he knew to find this special tobacco. He said that this was Sacred Smoke. Louise looked at me and asked if I smoke. When I shook my head and said, "No," she looked a bit surprised. I realized then that all Native Americans smoke tobacco, at least in their rituals.

"You have to smoke the pipe," she said.

"O.K., I'll be all right."

Louise nodded her head and smiled, her wisdom showing in those deeply inset eyes and the deep lines of her face. She was a truly remarkable woman who exuded such grace, such tremendous calmness of being that I found myself wondering about all that she might have seen throughout the years.

Patrick prayed to the four directions and, using a corn cob which had been lit from the fire in the center of the hogan, lit the pipe, calling on the ancestors and all our relations as set forth in the ancient tradition, smoking the pipe in the four directions. Then he passed the pipe to me and indicated that he would be passing the pipe around and everyone present should participate in the Sacred Smoke.

I took a few puffs, and was amazed at the lightness, the sweet smell and taste of the pure tobacco. The room quickly became permeated with the smell of the Sacred Smoke mixed with the distinctive woodsy smell of the pinion that was used for the fire.

Patrick took the pipe from me and passed it to the others on my right, first Mike, and then to Deanna and Ron. Then he carried the pipe across to the other side of the hogan where Dottie, Dawn, and several other family members were seated. They all smoked the pipe and it soon reached back to Louise, who was seated just to my left on a blanket next to mine.

Louise smoked the pipe with gusto, exhaling the smoke and patting it all over her chest and her entire body. She indicated I should do the same, as she handed me the pipe. I did as I watched her do, patting the exhaled Sacred Smoke all over my body. This continued, with the pipe being passed around several times until all the tobacco had been smoked, with Louise and Patrick doing much of the smoking. The rest of us certainly looked like the amateurs that we were when it came to Sacred Smoke.

As we smoked, the air became filled with smoke rings and mountains and other unusual shapes for tobacco smoke to form on its own.

There were many parts to the ritual, including my being touched with corn pollen on my face and certain parts of my body, and Patrick placing some corn pollen in our mouths.

At one point, Patrick handed me a crystal, which he said was like the one I saw in my dreams, and asked me to hold it in my left hand.

"This is like the crystal you saw in your dreams," he said. I was amazed. It really was *exactly* like the crystal Grandma had used in my Dreamtime visits. The same shape, the same width and length, and even the same kind of clarity. With all the different shapes and sizes of crystals he had laid out in a basket in front of him, I wondered how he knew this was the one I had seen in my dreams. There was no time to think about this for too long, because again Patrick was speaking to me.

"Louise and I are going to be saying some prayers. These are in songs and in chanting. What I want you to do, is think about your dreams and all the things that happened in the dreams while we pray."

He began chanting in his native language and Louise chanted with him. I was in awe at the rhythmic sound of their chanting and realized I had not been doing as he requested, but I had instead gotten caught up in the spectacle of this ritual. I caught myself and realized I should be thinking about my dreams as I had been instructed.

I closed my eyes so I would not again be distracted by the ritual and began thinking about my dreams and the various things I had seen and learned. I felt myself becoming deep in trance, a feeling not totally unfamiliar since I often attain a light trance state whenever I channel, but this was somehow much deeper than I had ever remembered feeling during my channeling.

I wondered if the Sacred Smoke could somehow be putting me in this deep trance state, since I was unaccustomed to smoking. I realized I was letting my thoughts drift again and brought back my thoughts to the amazing and wondrous things I had seen in my Dreamtime visits to a place I didn't quite understand.

I became aware of a voice. It was the same voice I knew from the Dreamtime, and she was speaking to me now.

"Rosalee, I am White Buffalo Calf Woman. I am with you now. When Louise and Patrick are finished with their prayers, I would like you to open your mouth and speak. The words will not be intelligible to you; however, please open your mouth and speak. I will speak through you. Just open your mouth and speak."

I kept hearing the same message, being repeated over and over again, the same way it is when I channel at times, but I don't voice or repeat the message I hear. If I don't acknowledge a message in some way, I just keep hearing the same message repeated over and over until I acknowledge the message.

I was deep in a trance and the chanting voices of Patrick and Louise beside me seemed somehow off in the distance. There was a pause in the chanting.

"Now, Rosalee, please open your mouth and speak," White Buffalo Calf Woman urged.

As I opened my mouth, what came out was not words at all, at least any which I understood the meaning of. I was chanting! Loudly, chanting things I did not understand.

I sensed Patrick turning to look at me with an odd expression on his face. Although my eyes are usually closed while I channel, I often have a sense of knowing whatever is going on around me. It's a feeling of being in another dimension and being here at the same time, but not quite. Anyway, I sensed he looked at me strangely as though he was surprised to hear my voice, but I couldn't seem to stop.

I was being carried along in my chanting by a power I didn't understand. I felt peaceful and knew it was good, even though I didn't understand it. It felt like I was chanting in this other language for several minutes and then I began to speak in English, but I wasn't the one talking.

It was White Buffalo Calf Woman, and I was channeling. Her words came through slowly and clearly.

"I am White Buffalo Calf Woman. I have been teaching much to Rosalee. Patrick, will you be so kind as to translate what I say for the elders to understand. I have been helping Rosalee much. There is much work for her now to accomplish in this life. She will be a writer of many books. She will bring our ancient Indian knowledge, knowledge of our ways, to the white people and to our people who have forgotten their way.

“I ask you all to pray for Rosalee that she will have the courage to go forward on the path that was chosen by her before entering into this life on the Good Red Road. There is much for her to do, and this knowledge she is bringing and will share, will help many. Through her writings, she will help to unite the people of the world in the knowledge of All That Is in the universe.

“Will you help her? Pray for her to have the courage and wisdom to allow her to accomplish this task.

“I ask you, Patrick, to translate this for me now."

Patrick began talking in Navajo and, when he was finished and it was silent once again, I heard the voice of White Buffalo Calf Woman again repeating in my head. She was saying something I had a fear of voicing, for when I felt it, I began to feel compelled to move, to get up and begin dancing.

"Now let us dance the Dance of Inner Peace," I finally repeated, though I forced myself to remain seated, sensing confusion.

"We will stop if you are afraid," was the next thing I heard and repeated. I sensed that this was not only meant for me, but also for many in the room. I was still deep in trance, although I was silent.

I heard Patrick signal something to the women. The next thing I knew was that Dawn and Dottie were taking me by the hand.

"Go with them," Patrick said to me as I opened my eyes, still feeling very deep in trance. I arose and went with the two women who led me past the door's ceremonial blanket and out into the light of day. It was a big change from the dimly lit hogan, and I started to become more aware of being in the present reality.

They walked with me back inside and I again sat down. They handed me a glass of water, which I drank. I had come out of the trance more fully. I turned to Patrick, still feeling dazed and confused.

"We were praying for you to have inner peace," he said. "Our prayers, the chants, were for you to have inner peace."

It appeared he was packing up his medicine pouch with all his belongings. I looked at him for an answer. I felt confused.

"What does it all mean?" I asked.

"What it means is that all these things have been happening to you and you are doubting them. Stop doubting. They are all real. Wake up and smell the coffee. All these things are real."

I just looked at him. I didn't know what to say. I still felt confused. I felt overwhelmed and I felt they must have all been thinking I was crazy, but Patrick said no more.

The Blessing Way was over and we laid out our luncheon feast. The youngest children who appeared to be about two and three were allowed into the hogan and everyone enjoyed lunch together. Afterward, we all helped to clean up and it was time to say our good-byes.

I hugged Louise and we thanked the family again for their hospitality and headed toward the hotel. Luckily we had requested a late checkout, because it was almost 2 p.m. by the time we arrived. We packed our things quickly and got back in the rental car for our long ride home to Deanna and Ron's.

It would not be until the following morning that the reality of the Blessing Way and all that had taken place there would set in for me.

The next day, I awakened with a feeling of calm that I had *never* experienced before. My breathing had changed. It was very relaxed and I was breathing much deeper, from deep in my abdomen. An extreme feeling of peacefulness permeated my entire being. I felt totally centered, completely at peace and at one with the universe.

~ 12 ~

White Buffalo Calf Woman

It would be a few days later, when I started to lose that feeling of total peacefulness and my uncertainty returned, that I again heard the voice so familiar to me in the Dreamtime. I was in the airplane on the way to Los Angeles when I began channeling, and immediately took out my journal and started to write.

"I am with you now in spirit, Rosalee, because you are troubled and confused about my telling you that you were going to see Louise at Spider Rock, and she would be expecting you and would know all about your visits together in the Lodge of Women.

"What I could not tell you before is that I am not Louise. I am a holy woman of the American Indians named White Buffalo Calf Woman. I have been here with you. I have been the one who has been your teacher in the Dreamtime, when your soul left your body and came to a place of spirit, which you know as the Lodge of Women.

"It is a place you have been to many times and in many lifetimes, as you have been a healer and a seer.

You do belong, and have belonged, to a secret society of women known as the Society of Women Healers. We are here together again, just as we have been here before. I am glad you recognize my name," she continued.

"From the very first time I saw you in the Lodge during the visit with Louise, I have been trying to tell you my true identity. However, it was not to be. You were not ready to hear and understand that you were, in fact, communicating and visiting with a spirit of a holy person from another time and place, Rosalee.

"Your consciousness blocked this every time I tried to tell you who I was. It just became necessary, if I was to be allowed to teach you all the things I have taught you in our meetings, that I let you think that you were meeting with Louise. She has, in truth and fact, been your mother and grandmother in other lives when you were also a Navajo and an Iroquois, respectively.

"It is with great pleasure that I am finally being accepted by you as who I truly am. Now you know that I am the Indian, White Buffalo Calf Woman, who has appeared to many men and women, mostly Native Americans or those of Native American descent, who have needed help and guidance. I can help you, and am helping you now."

Her message ended just as the pilot was indicating we were ready to begin our descent. I had a lot to think about, but things seemed to be making a bit more sense to me now.

I was eager to begin the California part of our trip, which was to be a combination of business and pleasure. Looking back, I had no idea about the types of experiences that I would encounter in the days ahead.

We took care of some business near Los Angeles, and had visited all the usual sites before heading north along the Pacific Coast Highway. We drove through Solvang late one night. The town was founded and is almost totally inhabited by Dutch immigrants who have kept their lifestyle even amid the hustle and bustle that makes up much of California. It is a place that time forgot and it was delightful. After leaving Solvang, we stopped for the night at a hotel near San Luis Obisbo. We enjoyed a very late dinner and went up to our room.

Once we had settled in, strange things began to occur. I suddenly noticed that I was missing one of the dream catcher earrings given to me when we visited Louise. I hadn't even had them a week, and suddenly I couldn't find one of them. That puzzled me enough, because I knew that when I came out of the shower a couple minutes before and looked in the mirror to brush my hair, I was wearing the pair. Now an even stranger thing occurred.

As I held the earring in my hand showing Mike that the other one to it was missing, the remaining earring felt like it was being pulled from my hand and it just disappeared into thin air. I searched everywhere. I looked on the bed over which I was holding the earring to show Mike, in the folds of the bedspread, underneath the bed, and on the floor, but the dream catcher earrings were nowhere to be found. I could have sworn that it felt like the second earring was pulled out of my clenched fist, slipped out of my hand, and disappeared like a magic trick.

Then I heard a familiar voice saying, "I gave you those earrings and I can take them away as quickly if you don't take the time to write down some of the things I wish to talk to you about."

"I've been on vacation and I haven't had much time," I thought to myself.

"I thought you were trying to learn," I heard the voice say.

I took out my journal and began to write.

"I am White Buffalo Calf Woman. I gave you those earrings by telling Dottie that you would like those dream catcher earrings she recently bought. I had been there when she bought them and knew you were to have them. These were the earrings I was talking about in the visit that you recalled when you were on your way to Chinle. I told you they would have a gift of earrings for you when you visited Louise.

"Louise was astonished that you knew what she had been taught when she was just a girl. She has forgotten about teaching her daughters and granddaughters about the secrets of life and harmony with All That Is in the universe.

"And there is a way for them to tell that you were telling the truth, my dear, and it is this. You were a bit afraid of telling what you had learned, as if you thought you might be crazy, or that they might think that you were crazy, which you are not, but in your shy and timid way, your honesty showed," she continued.

"Louise, first of all, knew this ~ that you were telling or speaking the truth of experiences, which you were not quite sure how they had occurred to you, but they had. So your sincerity was obvious to them and to your Grandma Louise especially. It is this timidity and insecurity that you must now lose. The ceremony of the Blessing Way has worked in helping to eliminate and alleviate these fears.

"You must know now that your fear of being considered crazy by others is not only totally unfounded in this life, but is also what you must now overcome. You must overcome this fear in order to proceed with your life's work of sharing the knowledge. The knowledge you had in the past, and also the knowledge that you have gained in your more recent enlightenment through your visits with me in the Lodge of Women, and the talks and encounters with your other guides. You will share this knowledge with many more than you could have ever reached in the past. And this you will do through your ability as a writer. You will write many books and share the vast and wondrous knowledge you have received, and now have to give. There will be many different books written, in different ways and approaches, to reach different audiences," she said.

"May I suggest that ours be the first book, the one you will write explaining your flying over Spider Rock and how it came to be that you and Louise met. Write about your meetings with me as you progressed in your knowledge during the Dreamtime in the Lodge of Women, and the things that are coming into fruition in your life.

"Include everything that has happened around your second trip to Spider Rock, and your meeting with Louise and the Medicine Man Patrick. How fortunate you are now, that you finally feel and understand the blessings that have been bestowed upon you. I am glad that this realization took place a day after you were in trance and I spoke through you during the Blessing Way.

"I am glad that now it is no longer necessary to let you continue to believe it was Louise you were meeting in the Lodge of Women. You are now accepting and willing to come face to face with your destiny, a destiny which you have chosen for yourself in order that you may fulfill your life's purpose of sharing this spiritual knowledge with many, Rosalee," she continued.

"And I am happy and pleased that you are no longer running and fearful of this destiny, as it is for a good and noble cause, and I want you to enjoy your life as it should be enjoyed. You do not need to be afraid of what others might think because all the messages you bring and will bring are those of truth. And in the new age of enlightenment in which you are now living, this truth will be seen as the truth and a message inspired from the God-source, and you will be revered and accepted with all your talents and abilities, and even with all your weird concepts. You see, in this new age, the weirder the concept the more contemplation it often inspires, as people are learning that truth comes in many forms and many messages.

And you will bring and are bringing several messages. In many ways it is the same message brought to you in many forms and disguised in many different ways, so that the experiences may be shared and will be related to on many levels by many people of many various and diverse schools of thought."

I felt overwhelmed by the words I'd heard from White Buffalo Calf Woman. I tried not to think about it, and just went to bed.

The next morning after we packed to leave and got into the car, I found both earrings on the front seat of the car.

"There are some things I don't know if I'll ever fully understand," I thought to myself, as I showed Mike the earrings, which had turned up as mysteriously as they had disappeared the night before.

~ 13 ~

Learning From Nature

We drove much of the day up the Pacific Coast Highway, stopping to see the sites along the way. By about 3 p.m. we were in the vicinity of the redwood forests and stopped at an old inn to look about a room for the evening. The pleasant woman who greeted us from behind the counter said that it was really bad timing, being Saturday, and that they'd been booked up for months in advance for this particular weekend. She was kind enough, however, to let us know that there was a reservation for people who had not yet arrived.

"If they don't show up or call soon, you can have that room," she said. We asked about a good place to enter the redwood forests and she generously offered that we might want to explore the private trails leading to a waterfall just behind the inn. We thanked her and said we'd be in touch to find out about the room.

Just then we realized we hadn't had lunch and were getting very hungry. We drove up the winding mountain road a short distance before stopping at a restaurant that boasted health foods. We enjoyed some homemade soup and light sandwiches. Mike and I were in awe of the beautiful scenery, which we admired through the restaurant's almost wall-to-wall windows that opened up the views of forests and mountains all around. Downhill we saw a beautiful home perched on a cliff above the ocean surf. It was at times partially obscured from our view by the mist, which was moving in from the ocean.

Tired, we thought this would be a great place to rest for a while and decided we'd really like to stop here for the night. Mike left the table and used the pay phone to call back the inn we had visited.

"No luck," he said as he walked back to our table. "The people just called to say they would be there in half an hour."

Our waitress was also returning to our table and Mike enlisted her help.

"We'd like to stay overnight in the area, but we've been advised that many places have been booked up way in advance. Can you recommend somewhere we might call for a room for the night?"

"I have a list of all the places in town. Let me make some calls and see what I can find. I'm sure there will be something," she offered.

She left us and returned about twenty minutes later. "There's not a room to be found anywhere in town," she reported. "Everything's booked solid. I'm sorry."

We were disappointed and tired. Nevertheless, it appeared we would need to visit the forest trail and head out of town before it got dark. The winding mountain roads were difficult to navigate at night, especially since we weren't familiar with the area.

Just as we had resigned ourselves to our alternate plan, our waitress returned.

"I just got a call back. They've received a cancellation at Pfeiffer State Park. It's for a cabin. Do you want it?"

Mike and I looked at each other. We were overjoyed! We really wanted to stay in these beautiful surroundings. "Yes, we want it," Mike said. She gave us the information and Mike immediately called to secure our stay for the night. With that settled, we felt at ease to explore. We thanked our waitress and left a generous tip before heading back down the road to the trail behind the old inn.

We started along the forest trail and almost immediately came upon some giant redwood trees. They were everywhere and they were massive. Some of the trunks must have been twelve or fifteen feet in diameter. There was one trunk with a huge hole in it which both Mike and I were able to go inside of at the same time. I thought how kids would love to run around among these trees, playing hide-and-seek within the redwood trunks.

We followed the trail that paralleled the stream, which we assumed flowed from the waterfall we could hear up ahead. The forest smelled heavenly from a combination of the trees and fallen leaves on the earth. My hiking boots, tied loosely the way I like them, somehow reminded me of moccasins on my feet. The air felt so clean, although it actually seemed a little damp, almost like a rain forest. Among the giant redwoods grew ferns and moss and a huge assortment of small vegetation.

What struck me most of all was the silence and the extreme feeling of calm which these giant trees exuded. I was just so taken with just *being*. Here, it felt like that was all that one needed to do. *Just be*. And it felt wonderful ~ peaceful, calming, relaxing and yet invigorating at the same time. The trail led high up into the mountain and it seemed to get more difficult to climb the higher we went, but we still kept going. Everything was so green and lush. About twenty-five minutes into the forest we came across a pond and finally, just beyond the pond, a small waterfall cascading gently among the rocks and small fallen branches and ferns.

We stopped to relax and meditate a while. I felt like I could stay here forever, but it had begun to grow dark and we knew it was time to walk back down.

As we drove the short distance to Pfeiffer State Park, the sun was setting in a brilliant display of oranges and pinks. By the time we arrived it was dark. We registered at the front desk and made dinner reservations before heading off to our cabin with some stacks of wood for the fireplace. At nights the temperature dropped into the high 30s and low 40s and we were looking forward to having the fireplace in our room.

We showered and got ready for dinner. After a delicious meal in the restaurant, with its view of the forest all around us, we went back to the one-room cabin and enjoyed the fireplace. It was the perfect ending to a truly wonderful day.

We awakened with the dawn and got dressed to go hiking. We walked down the hill to the restaurant for a quick breakfast. The air was chilly, but it felt good to be out in the early morning light. After breakfast, we were off again to explore the woods.

We walked through the forest trails, which led to a larger waterfall than the one we had seen yesterday. The trees were massive and I was awestruck. Everything was so natural and so special. It felt good to be so at peace, so at one with nature. The morning sun cast dancing shadows as it peeped through the tops of these giant trees. The majority of them appeared to be over eighty feet tall. The trunks had a diameter of at least ten to twelve feet, with many more that were much larger.

I kept lagging behind or going ahead of Mike so I could hide behind the massive trunks. I felt like a kid at play in the magical garden of the world. It was terrific.

First we walked along the forest trails, and then we went up the mountain trail for a spectacular view of the valley below. It was easy to get lost in just being in these magnificent woods among these elegant and stately trees.

It was almost noon, and we decided to head back to the cabin. The trail to the cabin led us again through the redwood forest. At one point when we had followed the winding trail and were almost within sight of the cabins, I just stopped again to take in the beauty that was all around, letting Mike go on ahead.

I found myself between the trunks of two massive trees. No one was around ~ just me and this wondrous forest with its age-old trees. They were so beautiful, so magnificent. Admiring them, I reached out my hands and rested my left hand on the trunk of the tree on my left and my right hand on the trunk of the tree to my right. I stood there in between, just thinking.

These trees have seen so much, I thought, have been around so long, I wonder what they would tell me if they could talk. Then, to my surprise and amazement, I heard a voice speak, as if coming from beneath the lowest of the branches, still high above me.

"I can talk and I would tell you ~ stand tall, be proud and spread your branches like a living legacy. The writings that you do are your living legacy. Spread the knowledge, share it proudly like the branches of our trees spread and leave a living legacy across time for all to see and admire."

"How do you know I'm a writer?" I asked silently.

"It shows in your aura, and in your thoughts and the way you view us," was the reply that came from the tree.

"You are a spiritual writer of the highest order and I can tell that clearly. Be proud, stand tall, and spread the knowledge that is your branches for all to see, and let the light shine through, and everything will be as it should, and you'll be admired as you admire us."

I thanked the tree ~ somewhat in awe and partial disbelief ~ and feeling more uplifted than before if that were remotely possible, I sort of skipped on down the trail with renewed energy and strength, knowing this was the vision which I had been told I would receive.

Advice that came from a wise old redwood ~ largest of all the trees on earth and hundreds of years old, this one probably having been standing here long before Columbus ever thought of sailing to "the New World" ~ and sage advice it was indeed. I was feeling stronger and more confident about my work all the time. It was a miraculous day.

~ 14 ~

Dancing in the Ancient Way

It would not be until mid-October, after we had returned from our trip, that I would make another journey to the Lodge of Women.

White Buffalo Calf Woman is speaking and says she wishes to clarify many things for me.

"We shall start with your grandma, your mother and friend over time. That is Louise I am speaking of and you have had all these connections and relationships with her as I have said. She has indeed been a medicine woman and teacher of many things in many other lives. She has taught you much ~ a great deal about the universe and the way it works. She has been your friend, and a healer, and will always help you when you need her. I have drawn you two together again in this life.

"I arranged the questions so that I might hear you share your dream of flying over Spider Rock. This was so that you and Louise would know there was and is a strong connection between you two, and so her family and Mike

would come to know and realize this was a very special connection as well," White Buffalo Calf Woman says.

The visit, or my recollection of it, ended rather abruptly and I knew from experience now that there must have been something more that I was not ready to remember, at least not consciously.

A few days later I noticed that I had been extremely tired. I heard a voice during my meditation and knew who it was. She confirmed this, telling me that she was White Buffalo Calf Woman. Her words were gentle and understanding.

"Will you not allow yourself just a little more time to assimilate all the information and experiences? Please allow yourself time to get accustomed to the ideas of the core of what your life's purpose is all about, and how it will be that you are to and will accomplish this life's purpose"

I guess that said it all. I had been overwhelmed not only by my recent experiences, but also by the things I had been hearing. I decided it would be best to do as she was suggesting and listen to what my body was telling me. I began resting a lot more than usual and took time to think about everything.

During the weeks that passed I channeled extensively, always the same guide, Jesus of Nazareth, and always he brought variations of the same message for me. That everything I had been hearing about my life's purpose and how it is to be carried out is very real. In order to help me come to grips with this, Jesus helped me explore some of my past lives through spontaneous regressions similar to those I had experienced with the help of my other guides.

I saw past lives that must have had an impression on my ability to accept and understand what White Buffalo Calf Woman had said to me during my last visit to the Lodge of Women. Until now, I had been unable to recall any more of the details. It had been a month and two days since that visit, but now the memory was returning vividly.

I picked up the memory of that night exactly where I had left off ~ in the Lodge of Women in the middle of a conversation.

"There is more to tell you than you may realize, my dear. Let me start by saying you are and have been a very good student ~ eager to learn ~ and you have learned well indeed. I am telling you this not to flatter you but to share with you and show you how real all your knowledge and abilities are.

"All and everything I told you, showed you and helped you learn and remember in the Lodge, each one and all the techniques and abilities are all yours to use whenever you are ready. These are your gifts and abilities across time and you have always used them well. Now go, will you my dear, and continue to relearn all your talents and abilities and use them to heal not only yourself but all on the planet as well. Indeed the entire planet will benefit from the wisdom and knowledge of harmony and oneness that you are here to share, Rosalee."

"Do not dwell on anything negative and always remember that the Field of Plenty always provides abundantly when we ask with clarity and give thanks in advance, knowing that our prayers will be answered. Go and enjoy this life my dear. I am with you always to help you continue to learn and grow and walk in beauty on this path you have chosen on the Good Red Road and be mindful that you are one with the light and one with All That Is."

I look at her face. She is smiling at me. "You are the woman that glowed in my dreams," I say, tears of understanding and excitement streaming down my cheeks.

She just nods in all her glowing radiance and says, "Yes, my dear, now you understand all that I have been telling you. Always remember to be a part of the light and remember you are one with All That Is, the Great Creator and all the earth creatures, one with the universe, a being of light and love. Remember this always, my dear Rosalee, for you have much work to do, and this you will accomplish well. Remember you are one with the creator, one with the light and one with the universe.

"Now go back to your bed and sleep and when the time is right, you will remember all we have discussed here in the Lodge of Women this early morning and it will change the way you feel about yourself in a more positive way than ever before.

"Then you will know the courage and will necessary for you to complete your life's work on this earth walk."

Then she looks at me and smiles, all aglow, and says, "Now go back to your bed and sleep and may sweet dreams be with you always. I am happy when you are happy. We will talk again soon, my dear, my friend across time. I am White Buffalo Calf Woman and I am the one who glowed in your dream with Louise, the first dream that you can remember in the Lodge."

Then the scene disappeared and I was back in my bed awakening. It was morning.

The next afternoon I decided to stop and take some time to meditate. I was all alone and the house was quiet. I lit some incense, carrying it into every room in the house, asking that only peace and goodness permeate my home. I walked back into the room I was now dedicating as my meditation space and shut the door behind me. Instantly as I heard the click of the door as it closed, I went into a trance.

There, standing in the room in front of the mirror, I began to dance and to chant. The chanting became louder and louder as my dance continued. At first I began moving in a small circle, then as the dance progressed, I noticed that what I did on one side of my body with my arms and legs, I automatically and immediately repeated with the other side of my body. It was a very balanced dance. It seemed I had absolutely no inhibitions as I chanted louder and louder as my dance continued. At the end, I crossed my hands against my chest and bowed my head. I felt extremely peaceful.

When I came out of the trance, I asked, almost aloud, if this was my Dance of Inner Peace, the one that had been mentioned during my Blessing Way. Immediately I began channeling.

"My dear Rosalee, I am White Buffalo Calf Woman and I have to express to you that I am delighted with your progress.

"You are growing and learning so rapidly. As I watched as you lighted the incense and carried it around your home to every nook and cranny, taking pleasure and pride in this sacred incense provided by our brothers the pinion trees, I heard you talk and think of inner peace and harmony. Then when you got back to this room you have so joyfully dedicated as the place of your meditations and a place for helping others, I assisted you in entering the trance state that you might complete what you had begun in the hogan of Louise not too long ago.

"That beautiful dance my dear was and is your Dance of Inner Peace. It is the same dance I was trying to show you and those who had gathered with you on the day of your ritual blessing, or healing as it were, the Blessing Way, which I told you about in your Dreamtime visit to the Lodge of Women with me.

"I am pleased that you allowed yourself to go so easily and deeply in trance in order that I might speak to you and those who were gathered at the Blessing Way that was performed in your honor. This honor is also an obligation that you, my dear, carried out very well.

"Did I not tell you that you would not speak with me again until during the ceremony? Did I not tell you that I am so very glad that you can communicate so well with spirit, and that I was and am aware that spirit talks through you?" White Buffalo Calf Woman continued.

"And you did diligently pass along this message to the Medicine Man Patrick as I requested, but you had no way of knowing that he would not fully understand.

"He did not understand as much as you would have liked him to, however, he understood and still now understands that you will be ~ you are to be ~ a great writer and warrior of harmony and peace. For this is your role as a spiritual warrior, and this is what the Medicine Man Patrick understands now very well," she said.

"I know you are not crazy my dear and he knows that you are not crazy.

"They are all a bit unclear as to what happened that day of your Blessing Way, but it in no way makes them think that you are or were crazy.

"They know Patrick was and is right when he said that 'You are doubting. Many things are happening to you and you are doubting them. The dreams, the knowledge, everything that is happening to you is real. Do not doubt it anymore. Wake up and smell the coffee. It's all real.'

"Then Patrick was more amazed by what he had said and the wisdom he had shown. That you and this experience had brought this out in him gave him pause ~ a reason for contemplation, for from where this knowledge or answer came to him, he is not sure, although he is most aware of the accuracy of these statements that he made to you that day.

"I am telling you this because you have now entered the trance state again, and have now danced your Dance of Inner Peace.

"This means that the Blessing Way has been successfully completed. By performing your Dance of Inner Peace so beautifully, so freely and so well ~ by letting your voice fill the heavens with your chants while you danced in the way of our ancient traditions ~ you have now fully been blessed with the inner peace which you so richly deserve. And you can and will complete the tasks you have come to perform without any further hesitation.

"I am pleased my child that you have come to the place of understanding within your being and that you can now share your joy in the oneness of All That Is in the universe without hesitation or regard for personal safety.

"Inner peace is and shall be yours from this day forward," she continued.

"I am sure you will share your gifts and abilities and your knowledge with the utmost respect and reverence for the Great Being, the Great Spirit who makes all things possible.

"Be mindful, Rosalee, as you walk on the Good Red Road, to be careful not to judge others who are not as enlightened as you, for their fears will be assuaged by the gifts of knowledge and inner peace that you bring. And that is your purpose, my dear child. This is what you have come here to do," White Buffalo Calf Woman said.

"And, by the way, I enjoyed thoroughly watching you do your Dance of Inner Peace. To open up that way is truly a divine gift and I am pleased that I was able to watch this occurrence.

"That is all I have to say for now. Do you know how pleased I am that you would open up the way you did? Well I am pleased in a way that is much greater than I can express. I love you, and we will meet again when the time is right."

I didn't know what I was feeling except that I was peaceful and I was extremely grateful for this experience and these insights.

It was the next day while meditating that the now familiar voice of Jesus came through again.

Again the topic was my life's work and he had a lot to say. He spoke about his time on earth as Jesus, and the fact that it would have been customary for him to follow in his father, Joseph's, footsteps and become a carpenter.

"But how could I possibly be a carpenter when I was to be a fisher of men?" Jesus said to me.

"I could not fight my destiny any more than you cannot fight yours, my dear. It is just this simple. It is how it is supposed to be. It is what you came into this life for and you will accomplish this very well," Jesus continued.

"As you heard the redwood say, 'You are a spiritual writer of the highest order and your knowledge is like the branches of our trees. This knowledge should be spread for all to see and enjoy.' Rosalee, my dear, will you not take up your destiny now and let your knowledge and wisdom shine like the sun shining through the branches of the trees?

"I am with you now and I am telling you that everything will be all right. You are not going to meet a fate such as mine. You will not be persecuted in any way. No ridicule will come to you and no harm shall you meet. You are bringing joy and goodness and light and only goodness and light can and will come to you," Jesus said.

It would be another couple of days before the realization of Jesus' words would begin to take hold. I awakened in the middle of the night to write something down. The next day, I read what I had written.

To meet my destiny, naked and unafraid,
Is the biggest challenge I shall ever face.

It was now 4:30 in the afternoon and I could again hear the familiar voice of Jesus.

"When you wrote that I was with you and I've been saying this to you for some time now, my dear.

"Why are you not listening when I tell you things that are important?

"Because I have been on earth before, I understand what someone has to go through when they make a commitment that will benefit mankind.

"Many may not understand what you might do or say. I am a very real advocate of knowing just who you are and where you fit into the entire picture as a whole. It is the center of understanding that will keep you on the path you have chosen when others may fail," Jesus continued.

"This is what you do not understand as yet my dear, Rosalee, that you are a part of a much larger and more significant movement that is sweeping across the earth plane at this time in your reality.

"I am talking to you about this for it is important for you to know that you are not alone. Many will help you, as I and we have said before. There are many in both realms that are here for the purpose of helping you achieve your goals and fulfill your life's purpose.

"I am telling you this now because the time is at hand for you to begin your work on a much more pronounced scale. That is, to a more far-reaching and wider audience than you have been sharing your work and your knowledge, for you are ready now to carry out your life's work. Amen. So it is and so it shall always be. I am the Christ, the one you call Jesus of Nazareth."

~ 15 ~

Talks with Jesus

During the weeks that ensued I began working occasionally with others, mostly friends, channeling their guides for them. I also continued to work on my understanding of my own purpose, and my level of comfort with these ideas and all that I had been learning from my guides.

I had been growing more tired all the time, and as a result, I found myself channeling less and less frequently. In late December, the familiar voice of Jesus came through again.

"It is sometimes difficult to understand that others may not be as open to understanding as you are, my dear Rosalee. By not being open to this, you are hurting yourself by expecting of yourself that which is not possible at the moment.

"You cannot rush the river, nor can you hasten the ripening of fruit on the vine. Likewise it is not possible to hasten another's growth and understanding. Each person grows at his own pace and, when the time is right for each of us, great growth and understanding becomes possible."

He elaborated on this idea for a while, and then offered a caution of sorts.

"A great big part of being enlightened is the ability to know when not to speak up and share your knowledge with others," Jesus said.

"When this happens, remember silence is golden, for you are affording others the ability to learn and grow at their own pace and when the time is right for them, and not before. It is a gift that you give, then, to those beings who are not ready as yet for this knowledge and growth.

"My dear, there is much more to understanding than meets the eye, and not everyone is ready to see what can be seen. Know that to these souls you can offer your kindness and loving patience and understanding. That is all. It is how it is and it shall always be thus. We all grow when we are ready to grow and not before."

I still couldn't shake this feeling of exhaustion, but the next day I spoke with a friend who explained what he thought was the reason for my tiredness.

"There is a lot happening in the universe right now, and people who are sensitive are experiencing this same kind of thing."

This made me feel a lot better; knowing there was some sort of reasonable explanation for what I was experiencing, and also knowing I was not alone. A couple of days later, however, I began to feel even more distressed by this constant feeling of tiredness. I had begun to have difficulty sleeping and I'd never experienced that before. I just couldn't make sense of it. Jesus began to speak.

"I am with you now to explain how many things are taking place all at once in the universe and why you are unable to sleep at night even when you are extremely tired and exhausted.

"Your energies are being depleted by the very presence of other planets in your solar system. They have a very strong pull on your energy. Many planets are coming into alignment, coming together at the same time. It is a great convergence of universal energy, if you will. This makes you feel weak as it stresses and draws on your energy," Jesus explained.

"That is because its fields of alignment and vibrational frequencies are rather close to that of your own when you are waking and, more so, at night when everything around you is quiet and still and you are trying to get some rest. And you need your rest now, my dear, but you are having difficulties because several planets are preparing to become fully aligned with one another and with your planet Earth.

"This is quite a rare occurrence that has affected and shall continue to affect your energy field for a while. That is why you are tired from the channeling with me at the moment. You are exhausted, depleted more than usual in your energy."

I noticed I was becoming more exhausted even during the time that Jesus was speaking to me. I also kept hearing part of the words and the tune to a song I remembered from my teenage years. They just kept repeating in my head, as if this was the easiest way for Jesus to explain to me what was happening. Over and over I kept hearing, "This is the dawning of the Age of Aquarius. This is the dawning of the Age of Aquarius."

Well, I guess I understood the correlation, but as far as I knew that "dawning" took place a while ago when the song came out. Anyhow, I was told, and would accept on face value, that there was some sort of rare occurrence taking place, an alignment of the planets that was somehow affecting my energy at this time.

Mike and I rang in the New Year with family festivities but I was too tired to enjoy much of the celebration.

Jesus had said this pull would be affecting my energy for a while, and I just hoped it would be for only a very short while longer. I was so tired it seemed that I couldn't accomplish a thing. I decided I'd like to go back to Sedona; somehow I felt the high energies there would help me.

It was now the first week in January and I had not received any sort of reprieve from this extreme feeling of exhaustion. I remembered what my friend had said about others also feeling tired and was somewhat comforted by the fact that I was not alone in this. As I thought about this, Jesus came through with another message, referring to the same conversation I had with my friend about ten days ago.

"The universe is letting you know to try not to rely only on the spiritual realm for answers, but to endeavor to work with and seek out the company of like-minded others. This allows for the experience of sharing and revealing to yourself and others the gifts you have, and also the gifts that can and will be received from others.

"Do not shut out others of the physical realm. Like-minded others are everywhere and you have to meet them and be prepared to share your gifts with them.

"A little show and tell might be in order, as with so many things on your physical earth plane, many people have to see for themselves; seeing is believing," Jesus said.

"This is what you have not been allowing yourself to do in Miami, but will be a lot more open about doing in Sedona.

"Performing in front of a crowd is only difficult if and when you are afraid that you will not be accepted.

"Know your gifts and abilities are to be well received and likewise rewarded, Rosalee. I am telling you this because I know that you still have a hang-up about accepting payment for your gifts and abilities, which seem to have come so easily.

"Let me say this to you, my dear. This is a selfish way of looking at things and it is also what is keeping you and us from going forward with your work, our work together," Jesus continued.

"Energy cannot be expended and not returned. It is just the way it is ~ how the universe works. I have already explained that most of the people with whom you will have the opportunity to share gifts cannot reciprocate the favor or pay you back in kind in any way for this gift.

"So that they will not be forever indebted to you with a karmic bond that cannot be broken, you must allow and encourage the repayment of a gift that they will offer as monetary remuneration in order to ensure that no debt will be incurred," Jesus said.

"Can you not allow this, please? Try and let go of this, one of your last and final fears ~ that of appearing like a charlatan by accepting payment for your work ~ and let's get on with the work you are here to do," Jesus continued.

"I am with you now my dear to tell you that I and those of us who are in the higher realms want you to make your living, and a very good living it is to be, from the gifts you have, by sharing your insights and abilities with others.

"This is your life's purpose and we have been endeavoring to explain how, now, at this dawn of a new age of enlightenment, you are to be a catalyst for mankind, helping to thrust the multitudes into a realm of greater understanding and growth."

Jesus continued for a while, talking about my growth and my life's purpose and suggested again that at this particular time, Sedona would be a good place for me to spend some time. He said, "The energies there will be more agreeable with you, Rosalee," and even suggested dates for my trip.

I was so exhausted I just decided to relinquish control, and agreed with the dates that had been suggested. I didn't realize it then, but I was headed for an amazing adventure.

~ 16 ~

Mysticism & Magic in Sedona

A week later Mike drove me to the airport in the height of rush-hour traffic. An early flight was chosen since I wouldn't be landing in Phoenix until six hours later. Deanna graciously offered to pick me up at the airport and drive me back to Sedona, where I would be staying with her for about ten days.

She greeted me warmly at the airport. It was good to see her smiling face and the sincerity in her eyes. She told me that her dear friend, Skip, whom I had met on our last trip, was outside in the car. Skip is a friendly fellow with a sincere and kind heart and a great big smile. He greeted me in his friendly manner and helped me get the luggage into Deanna's car. We headed out along the freeway. I was exhausted and the change of scenery lifted my spirits somewhat as we drove from the airport, the mountains stretching out in front of us.

"You've come at a good time, Rosalee," Deanna was saying. "We're having unseasonably warm and beautiful weather."

I was glad to hear that as I was never one who enjoyed cold weather, and I had a feeling that even their "unseasonably warm" would be colder than I'd like. The sky was blue and clear as we headed north.

"The weather in Miami has been awful, rainy and cold almost constantly for the past month," I told them. "It's so wonderful to see the sun and blue skies again. All the gray days in Miami were getting me down."

We laughed about the fact that I had to leave Miami and fly all the way across the country to find sunshine and clear skies in Arizona. It was strange weather all across the country and just yesterday I heard the television weatherman say that Arizona was experiencing the best weather in the entire country. It was good to be here. I told Skip and Deanna that I had been extremely tired lately and settled back to rest while we drove. About an hour later we stopped for some delicious barbecued hamburgers before continuing on to our destination.

When we arrived back at Deanna's after dropping Skip home, it was already evening. Ron greeted me with a friendly smile and a kiss on the cheek. I put my suitcase in the room and was freshening up when Deanna called out to me.

"I'm starting an astrology class this evening, Rosalee. Do you want to come along?"

I was tired, but thought it might be fun.

"Let's hurry, then," she said. "We should leave here in about five minutes."

I brushed my hair and got some water from the kitchen and we rushed back out.

The astrologer was a wiry woman with almost twenty-five years of experience in the field. The group was small, about six or seven women, ranging in age from their 30s to their 60s. They made me feel welcome although I'd only be sitting in on this, their first class.

The astrologer, Debbie, began explaining the basics of astrology, the houses, the planets and their astrological symbols. She mentioned something about the stellium, and lost me.

"I don't know what that is. Could you explain?" I asked.

"The stellium is the perfect alignment of many of the planets in the solar system. This only occurs about every three hundred years, and last night was the stellium, the time when everything was perfectly aligned with the Earth. This signifies a period of change, usually in the way of thinking, for the people on our planet."

Well, I was shocked and surprised.

"That's why I'm here now," I told them. "I was becoming more and more tired in Miami and I was told that it had to do with this rare alignment of the planets, and that the energies in Sedona would be better for me right now, but I had no idea this alignment was last night."

"That's right," Debbie confirmed. "But the effects will be felt for some time. We're moving into the Age of Aquarius."

"That's what I was told, but I thought that took place during the 1970s," I said.

"No," Debbie said, "We're just coming into the astrological Age of Aquarius. We're not quite there yet, but it's on the horizon. This is the dawn of that new Age, astrologically speaking. Maybe that's why we got the term new age. This is going to signify a new age, a new way of thinking."

"I have been told that we're in a new age of enlightenment and growth for mankind," I volunteered.

"Yes," Debbie said, the others in agreement. "That's exactly what's happening."

I was astonished. Here, tonight, these people had given me answers that further clarified and explained why Jesus had suggested this particular time for my trip as well as illustrating what he had said about meeting and opening up to like-minded others. I had only been back in the area for a couple of hours, and it was already beginning.

By the next day I had grown even more exhausted. By evening I was suffering from a bad sore throat and the following day, I awakened with a bad cold, feeling extremely weak. I tried some herbal teas and some relaxation techniques, but nothing helped. I had gotten sick, in fact, sicker than I can remember being in almost ten years, and even then, I don't think I felt as weak.

I spent five days in bed feeling like a terrible house guest, but Deanna and Ron were kind and generous, taking care of me as though I was their own family. I couldn't help thinking that it was quite enough for them to be so generous as to let me stay with them on this trip, and then I'd gotten sick, causing them a lot of extra work and more of their time and attention. It seemed I only came out of my room to nibble on a bit of food or to take a shower.

I tried my best to be sociable, and if for only perhaps one-half-hour at a time, I tried to spend time enjoying Deanna's company. We talked a bit about the things happening in her life and I also gave her a very brief synopsis of the essence of my experiences in the Lodge of Women and my channeling with my guides. I explained what I had been told about my being a healer and needing to learn many things in order to be able to share this knowledge with others.

Deanna made me a light chicken soup one evening, and a couple days later I felt well enough to accompany her on a walk in the nearby woods. Even that tired me out extremely, but by the next day I was feeling a lot better and stronger.

I felt as though I'd wasted my entire trip being sick but I still had a few days left and I wanted to enjoy them.

I asked Deanna to drop me off in Sedona's main shopping area on her way to work. She agreed. I thought it would be a good day to shop for a few things ~ some Native American music and possibly some gifts for Mike and my parents. The weather was mild (in the 60s) and pleasant, and the warmth of the sun felt good on my face. The air was fresh and clean here and I wanted to stay forever.

I browsed in many of the shops, buying some small items to take back home. After a couple of hours Deanna joined me and we browsed for a while before getting a bite to eat in a local restaurant and then heading back to Deanna's.

After dinner that evening Deanna had arranged to perform a spiritual healing for a friend.

"You can stay in the room while I do the healing, Rosalee," she said. I thought this a bit odd but figured that perhaps it was because I had already met this friend why she felt it would be all right. When her friend arrived, I headed toward my bedroom to give them some privacy, but Deanna called out to me.

"Don't go Rosalee. I'd like you to help."

"O.K.," I said, walking back from the bedroom. It was dark outside now, and the fire which Ron had lit in the fireplace was shooting its flames of gold, red and white, casting a lovely radiance over the entire living room. Deanna was setting up her healing table there, about eight feet in front of the fire. She usually performed her spiritual healing in the room in which I was staying, but the living room would do fine for tonight. She spread a clean white sheet over the healing table, laid a pillow at one end, and lighted the candles that were on a table nearby.

"I like to light a white candle and a green one," she said, reminding me of when we'd met. I had made an appointment for a spiritual healing during my first trip to Sedona, not understanding anything about what spiritual healing was all about or how it was done. I had some unusual experiences on her healing table that day, going into spontaneous past-life regressions and reliving some extremely traumatic experiences. Ron and Mike were as baffled as Deanna and I, since she had explained that I would feel very peaceful and relaxed during the healing. After that the four of us became fast friends.

Now I found myself with her as she was about to perform a healing on someone else. I sat nearby in one of the comfortable chairs and watched Deanna as she began to work in much the same fashion as she had done with me. She took a couple moments to pray and then, starting at the client's head, held her hands above the body.

I remembered the warmth I had felt emanating from her hands when she did this with me. The client appeared peaceful and calm. Deanna began waving her hands above different areas of the body, at times touching the client gently with her hands. She continued in this manner for about five to ten minutes, working reverently. She explained to me once before that spirit always guides her while she performs her healing.

After a while she called to me quietly, almost in a whisper from the few feet away where she was now standing by the client's feet.

"Rosalee, come and help here."

"What do I do?" I asked, getting to my feet and walking toward the table.

"You'll know," Deanna said.

I quieted myself a moment and then I held my hands above the client's head and felt my breathing change, similarly to the way it does when I channel. Immediately I felt a strange energy, as if it were coming through the palms of my hands. It seemed to pull my hands, almost like a magnet, and much the same way I do when I channel, I let this feeling, what Deanna called spirit, take my hands and move it where it wanted me to go.

I felt the energy flow through me and work on the client. At one point my right hand began making circles down the central part of the body. I heard a voice, one of my guides I thought, although I couldn't seem to tell exactly which one. He came through in a peaceful and loving voice saying, "Do you realize what is happening, Rosalee? You are balancing the chakras with your hands."

I was in a very slight trance when I heard my guide. I continued, feeling this strong energy permeating through my hands, carrying them, waving them over all the parts of the client. I got near the feet and noticed one felt extremely warm. The client had the ankle bandaged as though it might have been sprained.

I looked up and saw Deanna coming over toward to me. I didn't realize it, but she might have been sitting while I worked. Now she was beside me.

"What do you get from his feet?" she asked me.

"I feel this one in particular is very warm."

"What else do you get?" she asks.

"Just the warmth," I answered, not quite sure what she was after.

"Open up, open up psychically and tell me what you pick up."

I did as requested and the instant I allowed myself to open up, an image came to me. It was a picture of a man falling over a six-foot high pile of powdered snow. He could not have gotten hurt, but the thought of the fall frightened him anyway, as though the speed of the fall was what bothered him.

I knew that this had a symbolic meaning to explain the injury and I began speaking to the client. Out of my mouth came things I didn't know I was going to say until they had been said.

"You are afraid of doing your work. You have great spiritual abilities, but you are hampering your own success by physically creating a situation that makes you move slowly. It is a physical manifestation of your fears. It is because you are afraid of the consequences of moving too fast with your gifts.

“Lose the fear of using the spiritual gifts, and do the work you are here to do, and the ankle will heal. You are slowing yourself down, both spiritually and physically. That is why you have a problem with your ankle. Do you understand what I am trying to say?"

"Yes, I do. I understand very well, and that makes a lot of sense" he replied.

The healing work completed, I sat down, wondering how Deanna knew to ask me initially to help with the healing and then to open up to any psychic awareness that might be available, but I didn't ask her to explain.

I was beginning to understand that anything is possible in the realm of spirit, and I was pleased. It was a first-hand understanding of what I had been told in the Dreamtime about my healing, and it was an awakening for me ~ a true awakening to these abilities inherent in all of us by the virtue of our oneness with the universe, our oneness with All That Is.

The client left a few minutes later, then I asked Deanna to perform a healing on me. I didn't have any of the first reactions I had more than a year ago. Instead I felt very peaceful and calm, the way she had explained that it would be when I first met her.

Afterward, Deanna asked me to perform a healing on her, and then Ron came up from the basement and joined us. Deanna and I both did a healing for him and then he did another type of healing for us.

One at a time, we sat upright on the end of the healing table as he "felt the aura around our bodies," completing it wherever he may have felt any gaps or irregularities. This also was a very soothing, comforting feeling.

Afterward I asked if I might try this technique on him. He graciously agreed, and to my surprise I could "feel the aura," as Ron had said. It felt as peaceful performing this healing as receiving it. We finished just as the fireplace was losing its light and we all headed off to sleep.

"What a glorious day this has been!" I thought as I went to bed.

The next morning I awakened with the dawn and gazed out at the early morning light casting shadows on the massive red rocks just outside my window. They were not quite just outside, but it felt as though they were close enough to touch. Looking at them closely in the twilight, they seemed to have huge auras all around them ~ a bright white light radiating about the rock formations. It was beautiful.

When Deanna awakened a short while later, I knew what I wanted to do. Over her morning coffee and my herbal tea we planned our day.

"There's something I'd really like to do today," I told her.

"What's that?"

"I'd like to visit one of the vortex sites, the one with the large medicine wheel. Mike and I visited the vortex the last time we were here but didn't find the medicine wheel, and I feel like I really want to go there today."

"That's no problem. We can go this morning before it gets too hot. I know exactly where it is."

"Wonderful!" I said, my anticipation building.

We walked up the trail around the edge of the mountain leading to the big medicine wheel. A medicine wheel is a Native American prayer wheel built by placing rocks in a large circle with an X in the center, also created by placing rocks that extend out to the circle signifying the points of the four directions.

Group praying is a powerful way to access the God-source and send out healing to all on earth and for the entire planet as well. Native Americans have used the medicine wheel for hundreds of years to pray as a group.

It is my opinion that since at least one group and perhaps many have gathered at the medicine wheel for prayer, it makes the site a very powerful place for prayer and meditation.

Just beyond the medicine wheel was a cliff where one can really feel the energy of this vortex. I said a prayer at the medicine wheel and walked around it to the edge of the cliff. I stretched my arms out in front of me and could actually feel the pull of the earth energy. This place was mystical and magical for me.

I felt a need to lie down there on the edge of this big red rock mountain and just relax, meditate and listen. I had noticed that ever since I'd been able to hear the redwood speak to me that wonderful morning in California, I'd been able to hear the spirit in all my rocks and stones. They have told me what their purpose is and how they will help me if I am open to them. It's a gift I have been amazed at and grateful for at the same time.

Now I had this need to lie on the edge of this magnificent mountain and just listen to see what it might have to say. I situated myself as comfortably as possible on the rock using my jacket as a pillow and began to relax. It wasn't long before I heard the rock speak.

"I am here to offer strength and support. The rocks, these mountains are a high point, a point of contact between the earth and the sky. It is a good place to come and renew your earth connection and at the same time be aware of the divinity in all things. Take the strength, the energy of our rock. You give back to us with your admiration and when your work here is well done. I am here for you to come to whenever you are weak and need to renew your strength."

I decided it would be wise to do just that. Even though I was feeling much better, I still felt very weak and I asked the spirit of the mountain for strength. I lay there quite a while, taking in the energy.

Finally, after about twenty minutes, I got up and walked toward the medicine wheel. I again said a prayer and sat inside the medicine wheel, asking for healing. I sat there, laying my hands on a nearby stone, and in just a few minutes, began hearing the rock again.

"This placc is good for you. It is your earth connection. You have been here many times before and have always been invited back. You are on a road of enlightenment. Keep on the path, for it is here that you shall fulfill your life's purpose. Whenever you are feeling weak or depressed, think of this special place for you and you will receive the energy. You can take it with you, anytime you want, wherever you may be. Carry this place within your heart and let the energy fill you."

I sat there for a few more minutes, knowing what I had heard, but still somewhat in disbelief. My eye caught sight of a tiny pebble glistening in the sun, as if it was calling out to me. It lay about a foot in front of me. I asked silently if I might take this pebble home. The answer came back, "You are most welcome, Rosalee. It will help you remember your earth connection with this place."

Just then, I glimpsed Deanna walking back toward me. I picked up the pebble, giving thanks for the permission to take it and for the advice I had received. I got up, slipping the pebble into the pocket of my pants.

Deanna and I headed down the path. I was hesitant to tell her what had happened and the things I had heard, so I didn't say anything as we walked on down the path silently and I thought about what I had just experienced.

The events of the past few days seemed to more than make up for the lost time I'd spent lying in bed feeling so sick. This trip and my visit to this vortex point would be an experience I wouldn't forget anytime soon.

We stopped in town for lunch and ran some errands before heading back to Deanna's. This would be my last night with them and we decided on a quiet evening at home. After dinner I packed and the three of us visited until it was time for bed.

I went to bed, tired but still in awe of all that I'd experienced both today and yesterday. As I thought about these wondrous events, I heard a familiar voice. He identified himself as Jesus of Nazareth.

"I have some things to show you. Will you help me make things about the universe clearer for you? I will help you and you can help me by blinking your eyes ~ open and closed, open and closed, open and closed."

I did as I was requested and after what felt like a minute or two of this, I began to see a kaleidoscope of images all coming and going with the timing of my closing my eyes and reopening them, like flashes of a fragmentary picture. When all the fragments were seen, I came to realize I was seeing myself lying in the bed. The picture changed and I was now seeing myself as though I had been thrown across a floor, all curled up, and went headed toward a wall. I was seeing this in slow motion.

The most amazing thing is that I was hovering just above the floor as I was sliding toward the wall and then my hands seemed to hit a cushion of air that buffered me from being hurt against the wall. I bounced back ever so gently off the wall and then began tumbling back away from the wall. Again I was hovering on a cushion of air, and my fingers gently touched the floor. Unhurt, I bounced off and I continued tumbling gently.

After that, I saw what appeared to be a repetition of the entire event, only this one was not in slow motion. It was at a normal rate of speed, but it copied completely the pattern of the slower movement, and I was unhurt. Just then I realized the message that was being sent.

We create our own reality, and we do so mostly by our attitudes. If I find myself falling and think clearly and am thoroughly convinced of my ability to hover on a cushion of air and enjoy a peaceful ride, then that is what will be experienced.

If however, I allow myself to fall into the mind-set of our learned experience in this physical reality, then what I will experience is that I will, in all probability, be hurt very badly. It all ~ everything we experience in the universe ~ is a product of our attitude and our expectations.

The picture changed and became a series of collage-like pictures of which I was able to see fragments at a time. Each one showed how by my own thinking and my own attitude I, and each and every one of us, can create the reality we want for ourselves. It was a vivid revelation and one that I understood clearly, perhaps for the very first time. We create our own reality.

Now, I thought as I lay in bed, if I can only practice this understanding in my everyday existence, I can create the life I want for myself. We all can. It seems so simple, lying here in bed tonight, in this magical place that has already offered me so many insights

I knew then also, that it is a simple matter unless we choose to complicate it. We create our own reality, and as simple or as complicated as our life is at any given moment, we created it and we can create another reality if we wish. It was like seeing the world from an entirely new perspective.

I don't know how long all this took, but it seemed like perhaps a couple of hours had gone by. I was exhausted. I thanked Jesus and went to sleep, knowing the morning light would be arriving very soon.

~ 17 ~

Father Francisco Algetti

I had been back from my trip for several weeks and had still been experiencing a great deal of exhaustion. I was spending time trying to assimilate and fully understand all of my experiences in Sedona, and wondered if this had anything to do with my tiredness, or if I was still being affected by the alignment of the planets.

I was starting to feel more than a little guilty about somehow shirking my responsibility to learn and therefore be able to share what I would learn, but maybe I wasn't ready for it all.

About a month after my return, I began feeling much stronger, more like myself again. As was customary, Jesus came through addressing all of my concerns.

"Please remember, my dear Rosalee, you have not been nor are you being remiss with regard to your ultimate work for this lifetime. In any and each and every lifetime there comes a time or times of change, periods of growth and accomplishment, and also a time or many times of rest and replenishment.

"This is what you have been going through ~ a well needed time for rest and replenishment of the body and soul. The spirit that drives the wheel of life can only function well when it is alive and vital. In order for it to be so, often times a rest is needed in order to revitalize mind, body and soul. It is essential to the spirit of life, so you need not feel that you have in any way shirked your responsibilities," Jesus said.

Then he said he wanted to share with me some things I needed to know.

"I shall begin with the most important things first and we will get to all of the things you need to know as time permits. Will you let me take you on a journey to another life and time?" Jesus said, and suddenly I began to feel extremely sleepy and went into a past-life regression, which unfolded vividly before my eyes.

I saw myself as a monk. I was wearing a dark chocolate brown robe. Nothing covered my head and I had straight, dark hair that hung a couple inches below my ears, cut straight across the bottom. I knew I was about to die and I was regressing to my last thoughts of that lifetime. I was sitting on bench at a crude table, which looked similar to our modern-day picnic tables. As my final thoughts came to me, although I was in a mild trance, I reached for my journal and pen and began to write.

Blackness of night has overcome me and I cannot see my way out.

I am afraid of what I understand, and equally and as much afraid of the things I do not understand ~ an understanding of the universe that is very different from anything being taught in our day. Yet, I know its reality, and I know that I must go now, for I cannot escape the blackness that surrounds me.

It is time to pass on and see what I shall and learn what I must from a higher perspective that life as a spirit shall undoubtedly bring. And yet I am unafraid, for I know that in the darkness there dwells a light that shines bright as the sun for all whom are to behold and be part of the light.

I will endeavor to do what I can to return and aid mankind at another time, if it is thy will, the will of heaven.

Father Francisco Algetti will be no more than a memory, and yet I can see another day, when I shall come back in a new body and with a new name, to save mankind with the enlightenment of truth. And so it shall be.

I pray for All That Is in the universe to accept my humble apologies for having not completed my work, and when the time is right, I beseech thee to give this humble man, your priest, another try.

With that, I could feel the life passing out of me and all energy left my body. Father Francisco Algetti had died. As my body slouched over my journal, I knew that in that life I was an English monk who lived at the end of 1100s to early 1200s in Glastonbury near a channel.

After about a minute when the energy from that regression had passed, Jesus began channeling his thoughts to me.

"Father Francisco Algetti is but one of the many incarnations you have completed on the earth plane, my dear Rosalee. And I wanted you to see for yourself the thoughts that you had at the end of the journey of that particular incarnation, in order to understand that you are not a novice in the way you are thinking.

"Not only have you thought the things you now do and know about the universe some other times, but many times you have taught others as well, though not on the large scale which your writings are going to reach in this incarnation," Jesus said.

"Know you have the knowledge that is necessary, along with the courage and the will, and I am and we are with you always until the end of time, if there is such a thing as time. Know that you are not alone."

Jesus continued, talking about the need "to recognize and fully understand your purpose and the path you have chosen for yourself in this incarnation.

"I am here now to tell you, my dear ~ that although you are still not yet fully aware of the abilities you have brought with you ~ I am and we are a bit amazed that you were able to write as you were regressing and, in essence, reliving a part of another incarnation. We are well pleased to know you are able to do this.

"You have many gifts and we wonder how many we shall see in this incarnation of yours, my dear. I am well pleased indeed, that you are so open and allow yourself to experience the gifts you have brought with you," Jesus said.

This reminded me of the fact that all of us bring our own unique gifts into any incarnation, and it is by being open to them that they become fully integrated into our life experience. Jesus interrupted my thoughts.

"We have only just scratched the surface in terms of what we have to share with you, my dear, in order that you will also share this with many through your writings. There is much work to be done, and now I hope you understand more fully when I spoke of the rest you needed."

Jesus continued to speak of the importance of understanding myself in order that I would be able to go forward with my work.

It would be about three weeks later that I would again channel Jesus. He came through with a caution for me.

"Please remember, the time of your rest is not fully completed. You know this as you still have a tendency to feel tired at times when you think you should not be. Therefore, let things happen as they will and remember there is no rush for you my dear."

A week went by and I was still having difficulty meshing what I knew was my life's purpose into my everyday thinking. I was no longer feeling tired, and was encouraged that I could accomplish my work ~ at least I had my strength back.

The fears I had, when they did appear, were great and almost inexplicable, and I knew these had to be fully overcome in order for me to be able to do my work without any hesitation.

About one week later, Jesus spoke to me again.

"Know you are growing in this life and your gifts and abilities are unfolding as they should. Everything happens when the time is right for it to happen, and your gifts and abilities and the knowledge you will share is the same way. These are unfolding as they should, all in their right time."

Another week went by before I awakened feeling so exhausted that I could hardly get fully awake. I realized that I had been to the Lodge. My last visit had been several months ago and now I realized I had been there again. This feeling was like somehow not being fully back in my body, not ready to awaken, unable to feel and be fully alert. Later, after I felt better, I sat down to remember.

We are in the Lodge and Louise is saying, "I want you to know that I am glad you have come to visit with me my child. We have many things to discuss."

I look into her eyes and realize, as though for the very first time, that it isn't Louise I am with, but the woman who had glowed so lovingly in my first dream and who I now know to be White Buffalo Calf Woman.

"I am happy you are here to see and understand," she begins. "When I first appeared to you in a dream with Louise you reached out and touched my cheek. Upon awakening you told Mike that you had just had the most beautiful dream you have ever had.

"And now I want to make it very clear to you, my dear lovely daughter, about the connection and all you have been experiencing when you travel to the Lodge of Women when the Dreamers bring us together in the Dreamtime.

"I want to explain that I had much knowledge to share with you and still do. Your learning, your re-learning had to start immediately for the time was right.

"Your doubt and fear over who I might be could not be allowed to get in the way or to hinder in any way the knowledge you had to regain, Rosalee.

"I am confident that you understand this now.

"I am White Buffalo Calf Woman and I am your teacher. It has been this way with us through many lifetimes. You and I are members of the Society of Women Healers, and it is a good and worthy group of women who have shared knowledge and passed it along through many hundreds of years.

"We are together again now my lovely daughter and granddaughter and friend across time, to share our knowledge and learn from one another again.

"It is time for the healing of mankind to begin on a widespread basis. I am confident that you are up to the task of healing and bringing enlightenment to all of mankind.

"I will tell you an important story of how you have been extremely and successfully helpful in another time and place, Rosalee.

"You are a spirit who has returned to earth for the sole purpose of helping mankind, and this you will do very well indeed.

"I am talking about a life and time when you were a spirit woman who was known to the Indians as White Star Woman. You were at your best then, too, as you are, will be, in this incarnation.

"I am telling you this not to frighten you, but to answer your questions, make you aware of who you are. I am here to help you now as I have done before many times. When you were Hiawatha and I was your grandmother we shared many happy times together."

Just as I am about to ask about Louise's connection and involvement in all this, White Buffalo Calf Woman continues as if reading my mind.

"I will clear up the confusion you have regarding Louise. She has been a grandmother and a mother to you in other incarnations as an American Indian and she helped you then and taught you the healing in both lifetimes as well. I wanted you to have a name and face you would recognize in this life, so you would know there was a purpose for my being in that first dream with Louise.

"You told a lot of people to whom you mentioned this dream, that you felt Louise was somehow there to introduce you to the woman who glowed, as you had described me in this dream, Rosalee.

"And you were right. Louise was there in your dream for the sole purpose of introducing you to me in this lifetime."

I look at her and smile a big smile, with a little chuckle.

"I am glad you are pleased my dear daughter, my granddaughter and my friend across time. I am well pleased.

"I had to let you think I was Louise after that for it was a confusing time for you and you were not ready to accept the explanation, the understanding which I sent to you via the shaman woman whom you met. You were not ready to believe and accept the fact that I was a holy woman and as such, that I would have come to you in a dream.

"I had to let you, allow you to believe that I, the woman who glowed was your guide Kirstien, when in fact, she was the one who was on your right and the one who you felt or sensed had possibly orchestrated this meeting of friends across time. You always knew but were not ready to accept this simple truth.

"You had to be open in order that I might teach you all you need to know, what you had to relearn. Your guides, all your other guides and I, decided it would be all right just to tell you and allow you to think that it was Louise from whom you were learning, and your guide Kirstien, the one who had glowed and from whom you had felt so much love.

"You see, it was a little white lie we all conspired to tell in order that you would be comfortable and feel free to learn and regain all the knowledge you have. It became necessary in order that you may grow and be able to teach, to pass this along to all mankind through your self, your writing and your example. And we are all pleased, my daughter, we are all very pleased indeed.

"Will you not let me take you on a journey now, back to when you were White Star Woman?"

As I reached this point in my remembrances of the Dreamtime visit with White Buffalo Calf Woman, I suddenly became very sleepy, as though I was too tired to remember any more.

The thought occurred to me that perhaps my tiredness was a subconscious reflection of my hesitancy to be fully aware, to fully understand and comprehend myself or my own destiny, the reason for my being in this lifetime.

I paused for a few minutes, thinking about this, and then began again to recall the events of last night's Dreamtime journey to the Lodge of Women, or so I thought. The next thing I knew was that I was awakened by the telephone out of a very deep sleep. I had dozed off and an hour had passed.

Still tired, I tried again unsuccessfully to fall asleep. I started thinking about my writing. It had been only four days ago that I began an intensive effort to enter all my notes and my thoughts regarding my growth and my Dreamtime visits from my journals into my computer.

I had been stuck on how to clearly present a transition in my life and in the book, and now it all came to me. I quickly wrote it down and again tried to think of what I might have seen and learned last night about my life as White Star Woman.

The idea of my having been a spirit woman in another life seemed so far-fetched and yet I knew it must be true. This is the fourth time this has been mentioned ~ first by my guide Heidi, once by Jesus and now twice by White Buffalo Calf Woman. There must be something to it, but I wasn't ready to see myself as a spirit woman.

Unable to remember, I figured I would remember the rest of my Dreamtime visit when the time was right ~ when I was more ready to cope with all of me. For now, the writer in me wanted to plug the hole in my story with my newfound transitional paragraphs and I decided that's exactly what I should do. I went to my computer and began to make my editorial changes to the manuscript I had begun.

It would be four days later that I would channel White Buffalo Calf Woman.

"I am here to explain why you have only remembered part of all that you have been seeing and learning recently when you have visited with me in the Lodge of Women," she began.

"I know your fears and I understand them well. You are merely afraid of having been a spirit woman, with all that entails. Why are you a mortal now if you have been a spirit woman, and why would you have come back to teach when you are having such a learning experience in this life?

"I will explain. You have come back into this incarnation because you wanted to pass on your vast knowledge. This is what I have been showing you, talking with you about during the last two visits which you and I have made together in the Lodge," she said.

"When you are visiting again with me in the Lodge of Women, I will try again to let you see yourself vividly in your life as White Star Woman."

Two days later, I awakened with a bit of a headache and slight ache in the small of my back. This was unusual for me, but there was also that familiar feeling, a knowing that I had been to the Lodge of Women. I sat to recall my Dreamtime visit, but could not remember anything. Then I began hearing the voice of White Buffalo Calf Woman. I was channeling.

"I am with you now, my dear child. I am White Buffalo Calf Woman and I want to take you back now to our last visit, last night's visit in the Dreamtime when we were once again together in the Lodge of Women.

"I was telling you a story during which you recalled vividly and in great detail as your life as White Star Woman unfolded in front of you.

"You were not afraid then, in the Dreamtime. You were eager to learn and excited about this past life."

I began to remember.

We are in the Lodge and White Buffalo Calf Woman is gazing into my eyes as she is speaking.

"I have already given you an Indian name in this life, my dear, in your present incarnation, and the name I chose for you was and is for a reason. You are Golden Eagle With a Torch on Its Wings. Always remember this, and if and when you ever are afraid, remember this name I have given you, for this is your destiny."

Then she looks deep into my eyes, puts her arms around me and gives me a long hug. I don't realize it at first, but I have begun to cry, to weep uncontrollably. She keeps hugging me, and pats me on the back saying, "Feel the love I have for you my dear Rosalee, and it will make you strong.

"I have something I want to share with you my daughter, when you have finished with your tears and can dry your eyes. I have tried to show you this many times, but when you have gotten back to your bed and have awakened, you have not been willing and able to accept and remember the world I have shown."

She looks at me and I feel as if her words begin to weigh heavily on my shoulders. I feel weighted down and even a bit depressed, but White Buffalo Calf Woman just continues.

"I need you to try," she says. "Can you please, at least, tell me you can and will try to remember the things you are about to see when you are awake, have returned to the physical plane."

I look at her, and through tears, I say, "Is it so important, Grandmother? Why is this so important?" The tears again stream down my face.

"I can only tell you my dear daughter, that after you have seen yourself as White Star Woman, everything will be a lot clearer for you."

I shake my head in disbelief. I am still crying. Through the tears, I shrug my shoulders and say, "I don't understand."

"You will my dear," is all she says.

My tears stop and I suddenly feel more peaceful.

"Well," she says, and gazes at me with a gentle loving smile. I feel the love, the same love, and see the same smile, as my very first dream in the Lodge of Women. I feel at peace, though my eyes are still wet with my tears.

"Let us begin," she says, and suddenly I am in the woods, but it isn't Rosalee who is there.

I am a woman and I am all-aglow. A big white light, an oval of light seems to encircle my body and I am glowing. I knew that it was I, but I was somehow outside myself now, looking on at another incarnation.

I could see a figure of a woman in the glowing light. Her small size and build were similar to mine, but she was almost transparent, and the light, the glow, was brilliant.

I continue watching as this scene from another lifetime unfolds before my eyes.

"I am White Star Woman," my other incarnation is saying to a lean Native American man who appears to be about 20 or so.

"You have lost your wife and I know you are distressed. Will you allow me to help. I can help you, if you will let me."

The young Indian man seems enraptured by the glow of this spirit woman, as though he is somehow warmed and comforted merely by her presence.

"Know you are never alone," she says to him. "And although your dear wife has passed on to the Blue Road of spirit, I am watching over you and will be here whenever you are lonely. Know that your wife is having an interesting time in the world of spirit, as there is much she has begun to learn. She wants your happiness and will make your acquaintance when she can, but for now, remember I am here and you are never alone."

Then I hear a voice. It is White Buffalo Calf Woman, and it is as if she is standing beside me, watching with me as well.

"Do you recognize this man?" she asks.

"No," I say, again looking at the thin figure of a man.

"Look closely. Look at his eyes," she says.

The moment I look at his eyes I recognize him.

"Mike!" I say, looking at her in amazement.

"Yes," she says, "And you helped him in that life as White Star Woman, and you helped others, a great many others as well."

Then she points in the direction of the young Apache warrior and White Star Woman, and says, "Look, and listen."

"There is no need to be afraid," White Star Woman is saying. "I am here to help you, to tell you that all you want, everything you wish and hope for your life, can be yours. All you have to do is know that it is there for you. You are always in the bountiful Field of Plenty, and it shall always provide for you abundantly. Know this. And when you feel lonely, know you can change this too. Ask for what you want and know it shall be received."

He was looking at her with a gaze, a wanting to understand.

"Do not try to unravel what I am saying, for I speak the truth and you know this. Just accept it and know it is the way all things work," White Star Woman says.

"Happiness is found in knowing and accepting the way things are in the universe. By knowing and accepting the way things are, All That Is in the universe, you will find harmony, and this will lead to an ideal state of inner peace."

The young warrior looks at her, silent until now. "Will I ever see you again?" he asks.

"Whenever you think of me, I'll be here," she says with a loving smile. And with that, she disappears ~ just vanishes into thin air ~ leaving the young Apache alone with his thoughts and her words.

After that, the entire scene disappears and I am again in the Lodge, with White Buffalo Calf Woman looking at me expectantly.

"Well, what do you feel?" she asks.

"I feel a peacefulness," I say, "From and in every part of my being."

"Good," she says. "Now you are truly beginning to understand. And why is it, do you think, that you feel so extremely peaceful, my dear?"

I look at her and smile ~ a smile that quickly becomes a great, big smile.

"I'm no longer running from myself," I say.

She gazes into my eyes.

"No, my dear, you're not," she says, and we sit quietly for a few moments.

"I am at peace within me," I say, breaking the silence. "By accepting that side of me, the side that can be

and was a spirit woman, I now embrace all aspects of myself, good, bad, and everything in between.

"In harmony is the key to all healing. By being in harmony with all aspects of myself, I can be truly at peace and I will also be able to share this knowledge with others.

"I no longer have to hide myself, or any aspect of myself, from myself and others. I can truly be myself. I know this now. I feel it."

I am smiling as I look straight in front of me at White Buffalo Calf Woman. For the first time, I am actually seeing all of her, the way I had in the dream where we met in this life. And I realize that I have just gotten the courage to see her as she truly is and accept her as my teacher in all her brilliance.

"I am well pleased my daughter," she says. "I am most pleased indeed. Now it is time to go back to your bed, and when you awaken I would like you to remember our visit and all that you have seen and experienced with me tonight."

She reaches out her palm and touches my cheek and brushes the hair away from my face.

"I am always here for you, whenever you are ready to visit again," White Buffalo Calf Woman says.

And with that, the scene disappears and I am awake in my room, feeling exhausted and in a fog, as though I am only partially here.

After recalling this entire Dreamtime visit, I began to breathe more deeply, feel more peaceful than I had felt in a long time. I remembered the Blessing Way and my Dance of Inner Peace and knew I had truly connected with that place of harmony within my own being. I knew also that the way I looked at life and all aspects of it, would never be quite the same again.

I was no longer hiding from that part of me which knows harmony, understands the universe and is ready and willing to share this knowledge with all. I was truly at peace.

It would be about five days later that I would channel Jesus.

"Knowing yourself is the most important aspect of what you are here to learn ~ what anyone who is walking on the earth plane is here to learn," Jesus said.

~ 18 ~

The Enigma of Great Mystery

Almost two and a half months went by. I began going through a number of regression experiences in which I not only relived the pain and fear of many past lives, and was able to let it go, finally release it. I had visited the Lodge several times, each time to discuss matters of a personal nature, but last night the nature of my visit was somewhat different than it had ever been.

I am in the Lodge. White Buffalo Calf Woman is about eight feet away from me. There is a bowl in her hands, a mortar and pestle. I know it is her medicine bowl.

"What are you cooking up this time?" I ask. "What do I need now?"

"It is a mixture that will help you to make the right decisions for your life ~ what is best for you and for the purpose which you have come into this life to accomplish.

"Will you sit here beside me?" she asks, and suddenly I am seated on a wooden chair directly in front of her. I look up at her and she immediately sits in the chair

that appears as she begins sitting. She is now sitting directly in front of me gazing into my eyes.

"Grandmother, why have you been such a mystery. I cannot understand everything I need to when I have such mystery around me." I look at her, not knowing why I have said these words, not knowing fully what I mean.

"Reincarnation is a mystery in itself my dear daughter. And I know, you know by now that life itself is a mystery, and all the universe is a mystery ~ a wondrous conglomeration of All That Is. Why not be a part of Great Mystery, the very essence of All That Is in the universe? Is it not meant to be this way? Is it not our purpose for being?"

I look at her radiant face, trying to figure out where she is going with all this, and then I speak, with a strange understanding.

"It is an expression of enigma. All that is and all that will ever be is part of an enigma, the enigma of Great Mystery, and it is a great mystery of life."

"You are learning my child," and she smiles at me.

"And what will you do now with this knowledge?"

"Well, I don't know," I reply.

"Yes, my dear loving one, you know why you have chosen your life you are now leading among the people of the Earth plane."

"I know," I say. I look at her, kind of dazed, but also feeling a pulsating energy all around me.

"I am going now to share this knowledge in a way that all may understand, if they want to unlock the secrets of Great Mystery."

She looks at me and smiles.

"My child, you are ready for your work," she says, as she looks into my eyes. "Do not be afraid. I am and we are ~ all of us here in the higher realms who guide and

watch over you ~ with you always, helping to guide your path and show you the way."

I look at her and tears fill my eyes, not tears of sorrow or fear, but tears of an overwhelming feeling of being encompassed by such wonderful love. A wonderfully soothing feeling of love is radiating from her to me, such a feeling that gives me strength and balance and even clarity.

"I know there are many things you do not always feel you understand," she says to me, "but you are now fully ready to begin your life's work on a much wider scale."

"It is how it is, my dear. It is meant to be this way. It is all part of a plan of Great Mystery, and will all work out very well, as it should my dear."

She pauses, and I just look into her eyes feeling amazingly at peace, feeling totally at one with the universe.

"Your work is meant to be shared with many, on many levels and on a much wider scale than you have ever imagined my dear. And it is so."

I look at her still feeling very peaceful and we convey a mutual silent good-bye.

"Good-bye for now. I will see you again soon," we both say telepathically and in unison. Then she says, again without words, as they are not necessary, "Whenever you wish to visit, I will be here."

I felt very peaceful and calm as I awakened in my room, fccling tired, but with a sense of knowing, a confidence that I could and would accomplish my life's work.

After recalling my visit, I also sensed that the mixture she made up to help me make the right decisions would always be with me in spirit. There was a comfort, a sense of knowing that everything will be all right.

It was quite a while after this visit that I would again travel to the Lodge to meet with White Buffalo Calf Woman.

"Well, it's been a while my dear. I have been letting you go on your own now to see how you would fare. You are managing well my dear. I am pleased."

"It's nice, it feels good to be back here with you now. And what are you holding in your hand, in the bowl?"

"It is something of a surprise, a very special mixture to help you better understand how the universe works. You think I am talking in riddles, but I am not. This is a very special gift I bring for you tonight and I want you to take it and have it with you always.

"This bowl contains some of your wisdom and knowledge you have not regained as yet. How you use it will be up to you."

"I don't understand, Grandmother, how do I use, gain back, this wisdom and knowledge if it is in a mixture in the bowl in your hands?"

"You can start by knowing, by remembering that all life, everything you are experiencing, have experienced and will experience, stems from one source ~ the Great Mystery of life ~ and that everything also goes back to this one original source. Herein lies the key to understanding the universe," White Buffalo Calf Woman says.

She looks at me, the gaze of her eyes penetrating into mine.

"It's all one," she continues. "We are all one ~ the sky nation, the creatures that walk on planet Earth, the beings from other planets, and all those in all other dimensions, and everything that is around us, seen and unseen, heard or not heard.

"As you do for one, so you do for the God-source that is Great Mystery, and so the God-source replenishes or gives back accordingly to you.

"Are you following this concept, my dear Rosalee? It is of the utmost importance. It is the law of give and take, and every form of life, of being, is subject to this law of the universe. Are you following this?"

I nod my head. "Yes, Grandmother. Why are you telling me this now? Have I been neglecting this principle of the universe."

"No," White Buffalo Calf Woman says as she looks at me and smiles, becoming more radiant.

"We are all neglectful at times; it is a forgetfulness more than neglect. It is at the times when we need to remember this principle most that we sometimes fail to remember that we are one and all life is one and as we give out or expend our energy, so the universe gives back to us in return. Be mindful of this always.

"Now this mixture I have here in my hands is also a reflection of the oneness of All That Is. Even these ground crystals and bits of silver hold the key of oneness of the universe and they are a part of All That Is. Know this and remember your own truth ~ that you are a part of All That Is and only good shall come to you.

"Be mindful of All That Is around you and know that not all people are good. They are the blackness that allows others to see the goodness and light in you and so many others like you, those that walk in the light willingly and share their knowledge lovingly.

"As much as possible, stay clear of those who are not in the light. Let them be. They must learn their own lessons.

"Be on good terms with your fellow beings and seek the company of like-minded others. They will help to give

you the strength and courage to go forward with your life's work. Know all things happen as they should and this is meant to happen.

"Now I must tell you to go back now and get some rest for you are tired and will be working diligently this week finishing your first book.

"It shall be completed at the right time and everything will fall into place."

I awakened with a feeling of peacefulness, and like my previous visit, there was a sense, a knowing, that everything will work out as it should. It was an inexplicable sense of inner peace and harmony, a sense of oneness with All That Is.

###

About the Author

Rosalee Sirgany has been communicating with Spirit and the Masters for several years. She is a conscious trance channel and spiritual/shamanic healer.

Her gifts and abilities come from knowledge and wisdom gained through going within and understanding her oneness and harmony with All That Is.

Rosalee works with Spirit, allowing the energy of All That Is to flow freely through her being for spiritual/shamanic healing of others on many levels. Understanding and assisting others to experience the mind and body connection to All That Is, is one of her specialties.

She communicates and works with the Masters and Spirit Guides to assist others through communication and greater awareness and loving insight.

Rosalee channels and learns from Jesus of Nazareth, White Buffalo Calf Woman, Archangel Michael, Archangel Raphael, and many others.

Her work has taken her to various energy vortex centers across the United States as well as to other parts of the world, including the Middle East.

A seasoned writer and editor, Rosalee worked for newspapers for several years before turning her interests toward more spiritual pursuits.

Rosalee facilitates lectures and workshops on healing and spiritual and shamanic understanding, and holds private consultations as well. She is an ordained minister.

Rosalee is currently working on several forthcoming books.

Personal Consultations

Rosalee Sirgany has been named "Golden Eagle With a Torch on Its Wings," signifying the vision and light she is here to share. Her work utilizes multicultural ancient spiritual arts. She offers private consultations, which may be held in person or over the telephone.

Rosalee brings you the opportunity to communicate with your guides and the Masters through Channeling. Through love-filled insight, you can learn how to dramatically improve your relationships with friends and loved ones, find the career path that will bring you success and happiness, clarify your life's purpose and more. Hear the messages and feel the changes that these can bring about in your life. Truly an enlightening experience!

Through Spiritual/Shamanic Healing, Rosalee transcends ordinary reality in order to transfer universal light energy to clear the aura, balance and align all chakras and initiate your body's own healing response. Enjoy peacefulness and a sense of well being as you experience the universal healing energies.

To schedule a consultation with Rosalee Sirgany, please call 1-800-825-1553, toll-free.

Group Channeling Sessions with the Masters

Rosalee Sirgany offers Group Channeling Sessions for your group in your community. These have been called "Evenings with the Ascended Masters." The Masters determine which entity comes through depending on the energy of those who have gathered or the topic to be discussed. These are scheduled according to your requests.

"Evenings" in the past have included love-filled discourses from Jesus of Nazareth (Sananda), White Buffalo Calf Woman, Archangel Raphael, Archangel Michael and Kryon. The information is always given in a beautifully gentle and loving manner.

Rosalee channels these and many other Masters as well, so your energy or the questions or topic for the evening will be the deciding factor.

You may call 1-800-825-1553 to schedule "An Evening with the Masters" or to request more information. You may also get information through the Internet at:

www.goldeneaglespirit.com

Seminars and Workshops

Rosalee Sirgany offers seminars and workshops on various topics including Spiritual/Shamanic Healing, Opening Your Intuitive Abilities, Learning from Nature, Creating Balance in Your Life, and others.

In an effort to reach out to those who wish to open to the power of spirit within, Rosalee will schedule these seminars in your community with your groups. These can be one, two, or three-day events and would generally include a group channeling session.

For more information or to schedule an event, please call 1-800-825-1553, toll-free.

You may also contact Rosalee Sirgany by writing:

Rosalee Sirgany
Golden Eagle Publications
P. O. Box 161011
Miami, FL 33116-1011

Or through the Internet at:

www.goldeneaglespirit.com

Personal Note

I would love to hear from you regarding your thoughts or insights while reading this book. Your comments are appreciated. You may write to me at:

Rosalee Sirgany
Golden Eagle Publications
P. O. Box 161011
Miami, FL 33116-1011

Or contact me through the Internet at:
www.goldeneaglespirit.com

Please send your name and address (or e-mail address), so I can share any new information with you.

Love,

Rosalee

Look for these forthcoming books by Rosalee Sirgany

IT HAS ALWAYS BEEN THUS
A Revised Look at *A Course in Miracles*
This book, channeled from Jesus of Nazareth, is eloquently presented. It is the information provided in *A Course in Miracles* in a simplified form, with up-to-date examples for creating love in our world today, and miracles in our lives.
ISBN 0-9673597-6-7

GLIMPSES INTO THE SPIRITUAL REALM
A Collection of Aphorisms and Insights
This book provides understanding on various levels on a myriad of subjects, including friendship, love, life and death, understanding of our oneness with All That Is, finding our balance in our daily lives and much more.
ISBN 0-9673597-7-5

to let your spirit soar

Golden Eagle
Publications

P. O. Box 161011
Miami, Florida 33116-1011 USA

Phone: 305-595-4002
Website: **www.goldeneaglespirit.com**

Quantity discounts for organizations are available.
Call 1-800-825-1553, toll-free.